DWIGHT EISENHOWER

LEADERSHIP ▪ STRATEGY ▪ CONFLICT

STEVEN J ZALOGA ▪ ILLUSTRATED BY STEVE NOON

First published in 2011 by Osprey Publishing
Midland House, West Way, Botley, Oxford OX2 0PH, UK
44-02 23rd St, Suite 219, Long Island City, NY 11101, USA

E-mail: info@ospreypublishing.com

OSPREY PUBLISHING IS PART OF THE OSPREY GROUP

ISBN: 978 1 84908 359 1
E-book ISBN: 978 1 84908 360 7

Editorial by Ilios Publishing Ltd, Oxford, UK
Cartography: Mapping Specialists Ltd
Page layout by Myriam Bell Design, France
Index by Mike Parkin
Originated by United Graphic Pte Ltd
Printed in China through Worldprint Ltd

11 12 13 14 15   10 9 8 7 6 5 4 3 2 1

www.ospreypublishing.com

Artist's note

Readers may care to note that the original paintings from which the
color plates in this book were prepared are available for private sale.
All reproduction copyright whatsoever is retained by the Publishers.
All enquiries should be addressed to:

Steve Noon
50 Colchester Avenue
Penylan
Cardiff
CF23 9BP
United Kingdom

The Publishers regret that they can enter into no correspondence upon
this matter.

Cover image

NARA.

The Woodland Trust

Osprey Publishing are supporting the Woodland Trust, the UK's leading
woodland conservation charity, by funding the dedication of trees

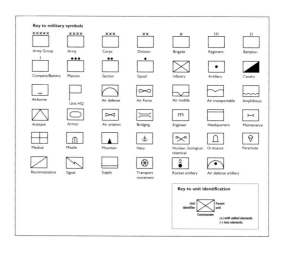

CONTENTS

INTRODUCTION

Dwight Eisenhower commanded one of the largest military forces in military history. Yet he never fired a gun in anger, seldom carried a weapon in his long military career, and was rarely within earshot of battle. Eisenhower came to command in an era where the size of armies had expanded so much that a new type of war leader was needed. While armies still required charismatic commanders who could inspire their troops on the tactical battlefield, they also needed a new breed of battle managers able to plan and direct grand operations at the upper reaches of command. Taking command in the industrial age of warfare, Eisenhower was not the traditional "hero on horseback" but more of a "chairman of the board." This was far beyond the role of a traditional staff officer, requiring a statesman's skills as well as an officer's. Eisenhower helped invent the leadership structure needed for joint operations by land, air, and sea forces. His most important contribution was in fostering the vital strategic relationship between Britain and the United States, which was vital to the coalition's victory in the war in Europe.

Eisenhower on a visit to the front lines in a jeep on November 16, 1944. (NARA)

THE EARLY YEARS

David Dwight Eisenhower was born on October 14, 1890, to David and Ida Eisenhower, the third of an eventual six boys in the family. The Eisenhauer family had originally emigrated from the Rhineland in 1741, and like many Mennonite families had settled in Pennsylvania Dutch country. Some of the Eisenhauer family used the English version of their name, "Ironcutter," but the more common family form became the Anglicized version: "Eisenhower." In the wake of the Civil War, Eisenhower's grandfather had moved his family to Kansas, near Abilene, a rough frontier town, because of the availability of ample farmland there. Eisenhower's father broke from many family traditions. In marrying Ida Stover, he married outside the tight-knit German farm community and outside the family's River Brethren sect. He also veered from the usual family path of farming, and after a failed attempt at running a small business in Texas he returned to the Abilene area to work as an administrator in a local dairy business. Both David and his new wife were exceptionally well educated for the day, as both had attended college. David was also the last generation of Eisenhowers to speak German at home. David was not especially religious but Ida eventually joined the International Bible Students, which would eventually become part of the Jehovah's Witness movement. Like the Mennonites, the sect was pacifist and the Eisenhower household was deeply religious under her sway.

Eisenhower had a quiet and happy upbringing in a large, humble family. The house was full of books and Eisenhower was especially fond of historical classics. He attended Abilene High School and graduated in 1909. Encouraged by their parents, the Eisenhower boys all pursued higher education and the brothers became unusually successful later in life. Eisenhower worked in the local dairy for two years to support his brother Edgar's college education, and in so doing became ineligible for the Naval Academy even though he passed the entrance exam. He turned instead to the United States Military Academy at West Point after receiving the support of his local senator. In view of the family's long religious tradition

Ike and Mamie during their first military posting in Texas in 1916 during the border troubles with Mexico. (NARA)

The "class the stars fell on," the West Point graduates of 1915. More than half the class became generals and many were prominent commanders in World War II, including Omar Bradley. Eisenhower is in the third row from the bottom, fourth man in from the upper-right corner of the podium. (NARA)

of pacifism, his mother thought the choice to be "wicked," but the family consoled themselves in knowing that it meant a free education at a time when the family could ill-afford to pay for the higher education of all their sons.

THE MILITARY LIFE

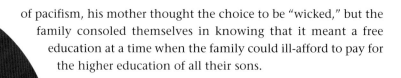

Eisenhower changed his name on entering West Point from his baptismal name of David Dwight to the more familiar Dwight David, largely because he was known as Dwight within his family. He enrolled at West Point in the summer of 1911, and had a short-lived career on the football team before suffering a knee injury. His academic performance was lackluster and he later described himself as a "lazy student," but he was exceptionally smart and able to pass the academic courses without particular difficulty. He got along well with his fellow classmates and developed a reputation as a particularly skilled poker player. His instructors had a mixed opinion of him, one suggesting that he be put under a strict commander in order to reinforce his lack of drive, while another saw him as "born to command." He graduated in the mid-ranks of the class of 1915, known as the "class the stars fell on," because of the high number of graduates who reached the rank of general. In part it was the luck of history; the class came of age during World War I but were still young enough to be active in World War II.

Eisenhower was nearly rejected for an Army commission because of his bad knee. Turning down an offer for a posting in the coastal artillery, and unable to get into the cavalry because of his knee, he accepted a post in the infantry. He requested a posting to the Philippines, but with trouble brewing along the Mexican border, he was sent to the 19th Infantry at Fort Sam Houston in Texas. He met the young daughter of a Denver businessman in San Antonio named Mamie Doud, and married her in 1916. Eisenhower had ambitions to join the Aviation Service, a career path the Doud family discouraged because of the high casualty rate among the fledgling pilots and the imminent arrival of the first of the Eisenhower children.

The declaration of war in 1917 completely changed the peacetime Army. Eisenhower had already developed a good reputation during his early efforts at troop training, and while he hoped to receive a posting to France, Washington saw otherwise. Promoted to captain and sent off to Fort Leavenworth, Eisenhower made a very favorable impression on the younger officers under him, one of whom remarked:

[He] is a corker who has put more fight into us in three days than we got in all the previous time here... He knows his job, is enthusiastic, can tell us what he wants us to do, and is pretty human, though wickedly harsh and abrupt. He has

Eisenhower's portrait from the 1915 West Point graduation album. (NARA)

given us wonderful bayonet drills. He gets the fellows' imagination worked up and hollers and yells and makes us shout and stomp until we go tearing into the air as if we meant business.

Late in 1917, Eisenhower was assigned to organize and train the new 301st Tank Battalion at Camp Meade. Expecting to be sent overseas when the unit was deployed to France in 1918, Eisenhower was disappointed to be sent instead to Camp Colt near Gettysburg to head the new tank-training center there. His performance in creating and training an entirely new type of formation led to his rapid elevation to the rank of brevet lieutenant-colonel in just seven months. His commanding officer praised him "as one of the most efficient officers I have known" and he was awarded the Distinguished Service Medal. In a rapidly expanding Army, skilled trainers were in great demand.

Eisenhower's next assignment was yet another sign that Washington regarded him as an open-minded and self-motivated young officer. The War Department decided to dispatch a motor convoy across the continental United States in 1919. The expedition was in part a publicity stunt to accent the Army's pioneering effort in motorization, but it also had the more practical goal of encouraging the federal and state governments to improve the national road network. The trip was completed in September 1919 after two months, giving Eisenhower a unique perspective on Army logistics. The shock caused by the death of his three-year-old son "Ikky" to scarlet fever on January 2, 1921, was the final push that propelled Eisenhower from a carefree West Point cadet to dedicated career officer.

On his return to Camp Meade, Eisenhower was posted next to another Tank Corps veteran, Colonel George S. Patton, who had commanded a tank brigade in France in 1918. Both officers quickly became friends and penned a joint article for *Infantry Journal* on the future of the tank. Both were warned that maverick viewpoints would cripple their careers; Patton retreated to his cavalry roots while Eisenhower absorbed the lesson that conformism was the way of the Army.

If the Patton–Eisenhower team would have significance two decades later, it was a lesser-known connection at Fort Meade that would have greater importance on Eisenhower's career. The wealthy Pattons staged social events at their home, and on one of these occasions Eisenhower met Brigadier-General Fox Conner. He had been General "Black Jack" Pershing's right-hand man with the American Expeditionary Force (AEF) in France, and was the intellectual force behind the AEF and a key Army intellectual in the 1920s and 1930s. Eisenhower's discussions with Conner about the future of the tank left him very impressed. When assigned to lead an infantry brigade in the Panama Canal Zone in 1921, Conner asked for Eisenhower as his executive officer. The leadership

"The man who made Eisenhower," Maj. Gen. Fox Conner. He had been Pershing's operations officer in France in 1918, and tutored Eisenhower in the art of war while stationed in the Panama Canal Zone in the early 1920s. (US Army)

at Camp Meade refused, deeming Eisenhower indispensible, in no small measure because of his skills as a football coach. Conner took the matter to Pershing himself, and Eisenhower and his family departed for Panama in January 1922.

Panama in the early 1920s was a tropical hellhole and both officers had plenty of time on their hands. Conner used the opportunity to tutor Eisenhower in the art of war, and Eisenhower proved to be both an enthusiastic and skilled student. He later referred to the Panama years as his "graduate school in military history." Conner was convinced that the Treaty of Versailles was so ill conceived that it would stave off another European war only for a decade or two. Although Eisenhower was far more fascinated by the American Civil War, Conner insisted that he understand the wars of Frederick the Great and Napoleon. One of Conner's most important contributions to Eisenhower's education was the importance of the "art of persuasion" in coalition warfare. Conner had been deeply frustrated by Franco-American command relationships in World War I, but he was equally certain that the US would inevitably be enmeshed in another coalition effort should American again be dragged into war in Europe. Conner recommended that in the future no American troops should be under the administrative control of a foreign army, but at the same time he recognized that coordination between the US and allied forces would be absolutely essential to the conduct of future campaigns in Europe. Conner served as a mentor for Eisenhower at a critical stage in his career, and he was later eulogized by a fellow West Pointer as "the man who made Eisenhower."

Ike's initiation into the realm of high politics started in the Philippines in the late 1930s while serving as chief of staff to Gen. Douglas MacArthur's special mission. They are seen here during a ceremony in Manila on October 23, 1935. The officer to Eisenhower's left is General Ulysses Grant III, the grandson of the Civil War commander and MacArthur's classmate at West Point. (NARA)

Conner returned to Washington as the new deputy Army chief of staff in 1924, and Eisenhower returned to Camp Meade. Eisenhower realized that if he hoped to advance in the Army he needed formal academic credentials beyond his impromptu education in Panama, and with Conner's help he was approved for the 1925–26 course at the Command and General Staff School at Fort Leavenworth. Patton sent him his notes from his own attendance the previous year. Eisenhower teamed up with Major Leonard "Gee" Gerow as study partners; Gerow would command the US forces on Omaha Beach two decades later. The Fort Leavenworth course was the Army's test for future general-staff officers, and the courses had been thoroughly reformed in the wake of World War I as a response to the obvious shortcomings in the preparation of senior US Army officers. In contrast to his West Point days, Eisenhower graduated first in his class. The Leavenworth approach to command was a source of endless debate between Patton and Eisenhower, which provides some insight both into their command styles and their future prospects. Patton warned Eisenhower to "stop thinking about drafting orders and moving supplies and start thinking about some means of making the infantry move under fire." Yet Eisenhower's focus on the managerial aspects of high command was the favored Leavenworth approach, and the accepted track for advancement into the senior command ranks. This divergence of styles helps explain why Patton's career stalled at field-army command while younger officers more in tune with the Leavenworth managerial style such as Eisenhower and Bradley advanced to the very top of the US Army chain of command.

After a short stint at the Fort Benning Infantry School, Conner engineered a slot for Eisenhower at the 1927–28 Army War College course. Ike was the second Eisenhower to reach Washington that year, his younger brother Milton being the assistant to the Secretary of Agriculture at the time and a frequent guest at the White House. Conner also arranged to have Eisenhower posted to the American Battle Monuments Commission, where he was instrumental in the publication of "A Guide to the American Battlefields in Europe." While a seemingly inconsequential post, the commission was chaired by General Pershing, who remained enormously influential within the US Army since his command of the AEF in World War I. One outcome of this assignment was that Ike was posted to France in 1928–29, where he walked over the World War I battlefields and gained an exceptional orientation to Western Europe's most blooded war path. On return to a staff position at the War Department in Washington in 1929, Eisenhower was asked by Pershing to review a draft of his chapters on the critical American battles of 1918. Eisenhower substantially rewrote the manuscript, and Pershing passed it on to his former aide-de-camp, George C. Marshall, for review.

A portrait of Eisenhower in civilian dress while serving as MacArthur's aide in the Philippines in October 1938. (NARA)

Pershing was Marshall's mentor much as Conner had been Eisenhower's, and Marshall was widely regarded as being one of the most brilliant staff officers to have emerged from the AEF. From 1927 to 1932, Marshall was the assistant commandant of the Fort Benning Infantry School, in charge of the academic program. He was impressed enough with Eisenhower to offer him a teaching post at Fort Benning. Only recently assigned to Washington, Eisenhower declined. But it was the start of an absolutely vital relationship. Marshall, like Conner, believed that another European war was inevitable and that the small peacetime Army would have to be expanded, probably in great haste. As a result, he kept a "little black book" of junior officers who he felt could take over senior Army positions when war arrived. Marshall's talent spotting was a vital ingredient in creating the US Army of World War II.

In 1930, General Douglas MacArthur became the Army chief of staff and he assigned Eisenhower's boss,

Ike and his boss during the Louisiana war games, Lt. Gen. Walter Kreuger, commander of Third US Army on their arrival at Lake Charles airport on August 11, 1941. Kreuger later commanded the Sixth US Army during the campaigns in the Southwest Pacific and the Philippines. (NARA)

Brigadier-General George V. H. Moseley, to prepare the Army's long delayed war-mobilization plan. Eisenhower toured the United States to visit industrial sites, in so doing developing a far better appreciation of American war potential than the average staff officer. It also put him in contact with Douglas MacArthur for the first time, and Eisenhower's growing reputation as a staff officer soon landed him in MacArthur's office. MacArthur was not especially fond of the new Roosevelt presidency and the numerous cuts in the Army budget imposed by the Great Depression. Neither was Roosevelt especially enamored of the haughty and vainglorious chief of staff. In 1935, Manuel Quezon, the newly elected president of the Philippines, requested MacArthur to become his military adviser to help create a national army. MacArthur's father had been the military governor of the Philippines in 1900, and MacArthur held fond memories of the Philippines from his childhood there. Likewise, the Roosevelt administration relished the opportunity to have MacArthur in exile on the other side of the globe. MacArthur convinced Eisenhower to accompany him as his aide, and, despite his mixed feelings about MacArthur, Eisenhower agreed. He served as MacArthur's chief of staff from early 1936 through the end of 1938, a period he later referred to as "slavery." MacArthur never served as the kind of mentor that Eisenhower found in Conner or later in Marshall; MacArthur was jealous and wary of talented subordinates. Eisenhower came to regard MacArthur as the polar opposite of an ideal commanding officer, and his own command style was certainly shaped by his experiences. One of Eisenhower's few consolations from his time in the Philippines was that he finally learned to fly an aircraft, receiving his pilot's license whilst he was there.

Although the years in the Philippines were a career dead-end thanks to MacArthur's disfavor back in Washington, it broadened Eisenhower's horizons regarding US security concerns in the Pacific, which would prove to be essential within a year's time. When Eisenhower returned to Washington in 1939 he was out of touch with the new power centers in the War Department and so instead turned to his West Point friend Mark Clark to help secure him an infantry slot at Fort Lewis with the 15th Infantry. It was a tumultuous time for the US Army. MacArthur's replacement, Malin Craig, retired in August 1939 and was replaced by George C. Marshall. Germany invaded Poland in September 1939, and the Roosevelt administration quickly realized that the severely diminished peacetime Army needed fast rejuvenation.

Eisenhower became chief of staff of the 3rd Division at Fort Lewis and became a colonel in March 1941 before being abruptly shifted to become chief of staff of IX Corps. Gerow attempted to entice him to join the War Plans division at the War Department, but Eisenhower expected that the US would soon be at war, and, like most career officers, he preferred a field position over a staff position. Eisenhower had developed a reputation as one of the Army's finest young staff officers and his skills were in considerable demand as the force began expanding. In the autumn of 1940, Major-General Walter Kreuger pleaded with Marshall to transfer Eisenhower to the Third US Army as chief of staff, and Eisenhower served in this position during the Louisiana war games of the autumn of 1941. Aside from his stellar performance during the exercises, Eisenhower attracted attention for his ability to deal with the press. The influential "Washington Merry-Go-Round" newspaper column by Robert Allen and Drew Pearson claimed he had "conceived and directed the strategy that routed the Second Army. [He] has a steel-trap mind plus unusual physical vigor." In the wake of the Louisiana maneuvers, Eisenhower was promoted to major-general.

Shortly after the Japanese attack on Pearl Harbor, Eisenhower was called back to Washington. The War Plans division officer in charge of Pacific operations had been killed in a plane crash in the Rocky Mountains on December 11, and Marshall desperately needed someone with experience of the theater to fill the slot. Eisenhower's new chief at War Plans was his old Leavenworth friend Leonard Gerow. Eisenhower had the magic ticket for the slot, not only because of his Philippines experience, but also his extensive work in Army mobilization planning.

THE HOUR OF DESTINY

The Arcadia Conference in Washington in December 1941, when the new Allies attempted to coordinate grand strategy for the first time, was Eisenhower's initial contact with Winston Churchill and the senior British commanders. At the time, Ike regarded himself as only an "unimportant staff officer," but Churchill, reflecting on his first meeting with Eisenhower and Clark, wrote: "I felt sure that these officers were intended to play a great part in [the war] and that was the reason why they had been sent to make my acquaintance. Thus began a friendship which across the ups and downs of war I have preserved with a deep satisfaction to this day."

Eisenhower's main task was to improvise a plan of action in the Pacific in the face of the grim news from the Philippines. He was dismayed at how the Joint Chiefs of Staff meetings in the War Department degenerated into "talk, talk, talk [by] amateur strategists and prima donnas." Peacetime procedure clogged the decision-making process, and Marshall was growing increasingly impatient with long-serving officers who had become stale. It was time for new blood.

In February 1942, Gerow was given his second star and sent off to create the new 29th Division. Marshall immediately moved Eisenhower into

Gerow's old position, essentially putting him in charge of war planning for both the European and Pacific theaters. It was a heady rise for a young officer who had been little more than MacArthur's lackey two years before. Eisenhower realized that he had been given the new position in order to instill a greater sense of urgency within the War Plans division. In quick order, the plans that had been suggested at Arcadia – such as *Sledgehammer*, *Bolero*, and *Roundup* – had to be fleshed out and turned into realistic blueprints for action. Marshall was quite frank about Eisenhower's prospects for being transferred to a field command. In the spring of 1942, he told him: "General Joyce wanted you for a division command and the army commander said you should have a corps command... Eisenhower ... you're not going to get any promotion. You are going to stay here on this job and you'll probably never move." Ike's acceptance of this role convinced Marshall that he would subordinate his ambition to the Army's mission.

Eisenhower's challenges began within the US military. Admiral Ernest King, the irascible Chief of Naval Operations, favored a Pacific-oriented strategy dominated by the Navy. This approach was rejected by Roosevelt, who favored the "Germany first" approach. Nevertheless, Eisenhower would be plagued with the constant bickering between the branches over the allotment of resources. To further complicate matters, the Army Air Force (AAF), nominally an element of the Army, was attempting to become an autonomous branch like its British counterpart, the Royal Air Force. Under its dynamic leader, Henry "Hap" Arnold, the AAF had been given a seat at the Joint Chiefs of Staff. The difficulties with the AAF were not over preference for a particular theater of operations, but rather over the enormous drain in personnel and resources needed to feed the AAF's expensive plan for a large strategic bomber force.

In May 1942, Marshall instructed Eisenhower to travel to Britain for the first time to assess the US observer group in London and to become more familiar with the UK's potential to serve as the principal base for US forces deployed to the European Theater of Operations (ETO). Accompanied by Clark, it was also his first encounter with Lieutenant-General Bernard Montgomery. It was not a particularly auspicious start to what would become an important relationship. Montgomery was brusque and impatient, and chastised Eisenhower for smoking in his presence. In June, Eisenhower reported to Marshall that he was distressed by the lack of urgency in the US liaison mission in Britain, particularly since Marshall was pushing for an invasion of France in 1943. Marshall consulted with the head of Army Ground Forces, General

Eisenhower demonstrated his formidable grasp of US security policy while serving in the War Plans division of the War Department in early 1942 under Brig. Gen. Leonard "Gee" Gerow (to the right). To the left is Brig. Gen. Robert Crawford. (NARA)

Lesley McNair, regarding whom he would recommend for the post. He suggested a number of older generals including Patton, Stillwell, and Fredendall. But Marshall wanted a younger man and so he asked Clark's opinion; Clark suggested Eisenhower, and Marshall agreed. In spite of his earlier promise to keep him permanently in a Washington staff job, Marshall was now elevating Eisenhower to a top field command: Commanding General, European Theater of Operations, US Army (CG ETOUSA).

Marshall's selection of Eisenhower was based on his assessment of Eisenhower over the past six months. Ike had demonstrated an exceptional grasp of the strategic problems facing the US, while at the same time his past experiences had made him aware of issues of national mobilization. Like Marshall, Eisenhower was a workaholic who coped well with stress. What separated Eisenhower from other planners was that he had taken to heart Fox Conner's dictum that "the art of persuasion" was vital for senior commanders. He displayed considerable political acumen when dealing with both subordinates and superiors, and his new position was going to be a test of his statesmanship. Conner had always stressed that "Dealing with the enemy is a simple and straightforward matter when contrasted with securing close cooperation with an ally." In Conner's case in World War I it was the French, in Eisenhower's case in World War II it would be the British.

Prior to his departure for Britain, Eisenhower took part in a Washington conference attended by the senior British and American commanders that was being held in parallel with another meeting between Roosevelt and Churchill. Marshall was adamantly opposed to a British scheme for an American role in the North African campaign. The British Army's art of war had traditionally favored peripheral operations, relying on the enormous strength of the Royal Navy to leverage the capabilities of a small and modest army. This had not changed greatly even in the wake of World War I, because the new Royal Air Force absorbed so much of British resources and talent. Marshall was concerned that the British strategic approach would fritter away Allied strength on a string of minor operations, to the detriment of the main mission of confronting the Wehrmacht in the heart of Europe.

Since the US was fighting a two-front war in both the Atlantic and the Pacific, Marshall was not keen on wasting resources in secondary theaters. He was unconvinced by Churchill's depiction of the Mediterranean as "the soft underbelly of Europe" and considered Churchill's preference for Mediterranean operations to be a "prestige" venture that was strategically unsound and likely to lead to frustrating stalemate. Marshall wanted

George C. Marshall, the Army chief of staff since 1939, had spotted Eisenhower's talents and was critical in Ike's rapid rise in command. They are seen here in June 1943 in Algeria while Marshall was attending the Casablanca conference with Roosevelt. (NARA)

a direct confrontation with Germany as soon as possible on the most feasible battleground, namely an invasion of northern France. Any other operations were merely distractions from the main goal. From a political perspective, the United States had little reason to support British imperial ambitions, and indeed there was a strong anti-imperial strain in US foreign policy both before and after World War II that was only partly suppressed for the sake of the coalition during the war. Eisenhower agreed with Marshall's viewpoint on these key strategic issues, but, more to the point, he recognized that he served as Marshall's executor in Europe.

Regardless of Marshall's assessment, Churchill convinced Roosevelt of the merits of Operation *Gymnast*, an Allied amphibious landing in French North Africa. It would provide an excellent opportunity to initiate joint Anglo-American military operations and draw off German strength from the Russian front, providing aid and comfort to the beleaguered Red Army. It exploited Axis weaknesses, especially the vulnerability of the Italians.

Eisenhower's main challenge over the next few years would be to attempt to bridge over these key differences in British and American strategic viewpoints.

ETOUSA

Eisenhower's new European Theater of Operations, US Army (ETOUSA) command was headquartered in the Grosvenor Square area of London. Eisenhower built up a small and trusted staff that would stay together for most of the war. His two closest aides were Lieutenant-Commander Harry C. Butcher, ostensibly his naval aide but in reality also a friend and confidante; Colonel T. J. Davis served as his administrative aide, though he was more formally his adjutant general. Eisenhower wanted "a son of a bitch" as his deputy and found his man in Walter Bedell Smith, known by most as "Beetle" Smith. Ike described him as having "a quick temper which he was wont to vent on friend and foe alike." Churchill nicknamed him Eisenhower's "Bulldog." A fellow officer described him as having "all the charm of a rattle-snake," with an irascible temperament fostered by his diet of "cigarettes, bourbon and Dexadrine." Smith was a critical element in Eisenhower's command team, and became his alter ego. While Ike preferred to persuade and was reluctant to impose his will, Smith was notoriously short-tempered and assertive. Smith served as Ike's hatchet man, undertaking tasks that Eisenhower was reluctant to do. Unlike many other senior American commanders in the Mediterranean theater, he was adept at working with the British, an essential virtue in Eisenhower's universe.

Ike and Churchill became acquainted during his first stint in England with the ETOUSA command in 1942. Here they are seen in Ike's command trailer in November 1944. (NARA)

Churchill had struck up a quick friendship with Eisenhower, inviting him to 10 Downing Street and to Chequers, his country home. Churchill recognized Eisenhower as another means to influence American policy. Having served under MacArthur, Ike had enough experience with egotistical leaders, but found that Churchill counterbalanced his frequent bullying and interminable monologues with charm and grace. Both men shared a fondness for military history, which served as a comfortable retreat from Churchill's frequent promotions of his latest military schemes. Eisenhower was honored by Churchill's cordiality and fully appreciated the value of having the prime minister's ear.

Agreement on an initial Allied course of action came in July 1942. Marshall, Eisenhower, King, and Harry Hopkins, Roosevelt's personal representative, met along with their British counterparts to hammer out the first joint operations. The American position was fatally weakened by its disharmony. Marshall and Eisenhower pushed for an early invasion of France using Operation *Sledgehammer*, King pushed for greater priority in the Pacific, and Hopkins accepted the British proposal for Operation *Gymnast* in the Mediterranean. *Sledgehammer* was envisioned as a limited operation in Brittany or the Cotentin peninsula of Normandy that would seize a lodgment area and hold it until the main Allied landing, codenamed *Roundup*, could be staged. The British delegation pointed out that the Allies lacked the landing craft to conduct Operation *Sledgehammer* and that until the US Army presence in Britain was substantially enlarged, any Allied landing force would be grossly outnumbered by the Wehrmacht. The operation was "dead on arrival" and both Eisenhower and Marshall were forced to concede that the North African mission was the "least harmful." Operation *Gymnast*, renamed Operation *Torch* in its final form, was scheduled for November 1942. The disastrous British–Canadian landing at Dieppe on August 19, 1942, suggested how far the Allies had to go before staging a major amphibious landing in France.

The *Torch* plan eventually involved the amphibious landings of US forces on the French North African coast in Morocco and Algeria; British participation in the first waves was ruled out in view of the animosity between the British and French after the Royal Navy had sunk the French fleet in North Africa at Mers-el-Kebir in 1940 to prevent it from falling into German hands. Aside from offering a lodgment in North Africa, Marshall and Eisenhower also hoped that it might bring part of the French Army back into the Allied fold, and there were extensive efforts made to convince the French Army of Africa to switch sides even before the landings, led by Clark. The American landings were based on the premise that the French

Eisenhower recruited his old friend Harry Butcher to serve as his aide-de-camp during the war, though Butcher was officially designated as his naval aide. Butcher's wife and Mamie Eisenhower shared an apartment in Washington during the war. (NARA)

would not resist, or at worst would offer only a token resistance. Once the lodgment was secured, the plan was to squeeze out the remaining German and Italian forces in North Africa by a joint British–American force pushing eastward to join up in Tunisia with Montgomery's Eighth Army, which was moving westward after its victory at El Alamein.

AFHQ

The decision to appoint an American as the supreme commander for Operation *Torch* was made by the Combined Chiefs of Staff (CCS) on July 25, 1942, based on Churchill's recommendation. As the official Allied Forces Headquarters (AFHQ) history later noted: "The initial invasion had to have the appearance of being an American enterprise because of French bitterness (however unjustifiable) toward the British after Dunkirk and Mers-el-Kebir." The position of supreme commander was directly subordinate to the CCS. Eisenhower, who had been promoted to lieutenant-general on July 7, 1942, prior to being dispatched to ETOUSA in London, was tentatively designated to this post in addition to his ETOUSA command during the CCS meeting, and it was formally announced on September 12, 1942. His deputy supreme commander was Clark, based on Eisenhower's recommendation. This was in violation of the later practice of balancing an American command position with a British one, but it was done in the *Torch* case to maintain the pretense that the operation was only American. The new joint command was designated as AFHQ (Allied Forces Headquarters).

AFHQ was the test bed for future joint operations and served to iron out British and American differences in command practices as well as creating a joint working environment. Eisenhower went to great lengths trying to foster unity of command and attempted to submerge national interference in command decisions except in exceptional cases. British and American command styles differed, which led to misunderstandings. American commanders had their staff prepare options and then selected a plan from these; British commanders selected a course of action and then had their staff work out the details.

Eisenhower's AFHQ command not only had to bridge the divergent viewpoints of the British and American sides, but it also had to harmonize the actions of the three combat services (air, land, and sea) of both sides as well as the logistical and administrative infrastructure. The task was undoubtedly aided by the common English language between both sides, in contrast to the difficulties between US and French command structures in 1918. The differences between British and American English are often exaggerated, and the AFHQ history later noted that it proved to be an advantage rather than an obstacle: "The good natured banter exchanged regarding each other's peculiarities often served to ease tensions rather than create them." Indeed, a later General Board study of the ETOUSA experience underlined the advantages of the common language and noted that it probably would not have been possible to so closely integrate the operations of both sides without this advantage.

Mediterranean Theater of Operations

YUGOSLAVIA

ADRIATIC SEA

Foggia

Naples

Salerno

Operation *Baytown*, September 3, 1943

Messina

Sicily

Malta

SEA

Tripoli

TRIPOLITANIA

Rome

Anzio

Operation *Avalanche*, Sepember 9, 1943

Operation *Husky*, July 10, 1943

ITALY

Operation *Shingle*, January 22, 1944

La Marsa

Tunis

Final Allied offensive, April–May, 1942

Corsica

Sardinia

M E D I T E R R A N E A N

Race for Tunis, November–December, 1942

Bône

TUNISIA

Kasserine Pass, February 14–22, 1943

Marseille

Balearic Islands

Operation *Torch*, November 8, 1942

Algiers

Mostaganem

N

ALGERIA

Operation *Torch*, November 8, 1942

Oran

FRANCE

Madrid

SPAIN

Gibraltar

SPANISH MOROCCO

PORTUGAL

Rabat

Casablanca

FRENCH MOROCCO

Operation *Torch*, November 8, 1942

Marrakesh

200 miles

200km

0

0

17

Eisenhower set up a temporary headquarters in Gibraltar when Operation *Torch* was launched on November 8, 1942. The landings were successful and encountered short but heated French resistance. Clark continued his negotiations with the Vichy French leaders, and finally convinced Admiral Jean Darlan to accept a ceasefire under which the French colonial regime remained in power, though switched sides. The Darlan deal raised a stink in the United States because of the dim popular view of Vichy French collaborationism, but calls for Eisenhower's replacement were squashed by Roosevelt, who recognized Eisenhower's actions as a shrewd political deal for French cooperation based on pragmatic grounds and not any ideological sympathy.

Even though the landings had gone about as well as could be expected, the follow-up operations to push into Tunisia were hampered by the difficulties of logistics on such an extended front. The German Mediterranean commander, Albert Kesselring, realized that Tunisia held the key to the Mediterranean campaign, and not only began steps to deploy Arnim's 5. Panzerarmee to Tunisia to reinforce Rommel's Italian–German forces, but he also shifted Luftwaffe resources to airfields in Sicily in order to ensure Axis air superiority. The ensuing Tunisian campaign was Eisenhower's most troubled endeavor as the Allies learned to fight joint campaigns, and Ike learned how to deal with the British. Eisenhower's inexperience in command, the novelty of a new joint command dominated by British officers, and his divided responsibilities resulted in weak and distracted leadership. Eisenhower was still nominally the NATOUSA (North African Theater of Operations, US Army) commander whilst also commanding AFHQ. The command structure lacked sufficient subordinate layers to help focus the US Army effort.

Under the July 1942 agreement, the Tunisian land operation was led by a British commander, Lieutenant-General Kenneth Anderson, whose First Army contained the American contingent, II Corps under Major-General Lloyd Fredendall. Although Fredendall had been among a small group of officers singled out by Marshall for senior combat commands, he proved to be the worst of all senior American commanders in the war. Anderson deployed Fredendall's corps over too wide an expanse of Tunisian hill country and misread signals-intelligence information regarding German intentions. Anderson anticipated that the German counterattack in early 1943 would fall against the British corps in northern Tunisia instead of Fredendall's over-extended corps in the Western Dorsal mountains in southern Tunisia, and so reinforced the wrong sector. Eisenhower visited the front in early February and was dismayed by the disposition of Fredendall's command. Before he was able to impose changes, the Germans struck.

The Germans thought the inexperienced Americans were a more vulnerable target, and staged a mid-February attack towards Kasserine Pass that overran a number of American units. Even though the German attack was quickly stopped, it severely undermined the reputation of the US Army in British eyes. Aside from poor tactical decision-making, the Allied forces in Tunisia worked under the handicap of poor air support. Eisenhower attempted to retain operational control through the AFHQ in Algiers, and influenced the tactical command through a forward headquarters at Constantine. He began to appreciate the need to delegate more authority, and called in Lucien Truscott to serve as his surrogate in Algiers while he was away at the front. But the Kasserine Pass battles suggested that more extensive changes were needed.

A series of organizational changes occurred in early 1943 that further refined Anglo-American joint operations. With the forthcoming juncture of Anderson's First Army and Montgomery's Eighth Army in Tunisia, an additional level of operational command below Eisenhower seemed prudent. General Harold Alexander, previously the British commander-in-chief of the Middle East, became the commander of the newly formed 18th Army Group to direct the First and Eighth Armies. Simultaneously, Alexander became Deputy commander-in-chief of Allied forces in North Africa, paralleling the air and naval theater commands, and Clark was redeployed to command the new Fifth US Army. This returned the senior command positions to the practice of having a Briton and American share the roles of commander and deputy. The experiences in Tunisia would help create the command structure used later in the war in northwest Europe.

The Kasserine Pass debacle also led to a shake-up among the American commanders. Eisenhower relieved Fredendall and called in Patton from his I Armored Corps command in Algeria to take over II Corps in Tunisia. Eisenhower attempted to place his West Point classmate Omar Bradley in Patton's headquarters as his representative, but Patton insisted on a more regular command arrangement, not wanting Bradley to serve as "Eisenhower's spy." When Patton was pulled out of Tunisia prior to the end of the campaign to take over the new Seventh US Army being organized for the invasion of Sicily, Bradley became the corps' commander. Besides giving the US Army a great deal of practical experience in the realities of modern warfare, Tunisia also helped to sort out the tactical commanders. Reputations were won and lost, and a cadre of senior commanders at corps and army level began to emerge. Subordinating Fredendall's corps to Anderson's British field army had been a mistake, primarily because of the fundamental differences in tactical doctrine in both armies; it had been an expedient solution and against the practices recommended since the AEF days of 1918. It would not be repeated after Tunisia except in extraordinary circumstances. From this point on, US forces, with rare exceptions, would fight within their own field armies, and would seldom be subordinated to British units in units of corps size or below.

After the Kasserine Pass debacle, Eisenhower turned to Clark to take over the troubled II Corps. When he refused, Eisenhower turned to his old friend George Patton, and they are seen here in Patton's office in Tunisia on March 16, 1943, talking about the forthcoming campaign. (NARA)

For all the bickering, backstabbing, and arguments, Britain and the United States had won their first joint campaign under Eisenhower's command. The quality of senior British leadership in the Mediterranean was excellent, and Eisenhower attempted to keep together the Mediterranean team in the subsequent operations in France. The one exception was Anderson, who was shunted off after the Kasserine Pass fiasco. Eisenhower had enormous respect for Alexander, and thought Admiral "ABC" Cunningham a sea warrior "of the Nelsonian cut." Eisenhower was comfortable working with Tedder and would later turn to him in the campaign in northwest Europe. Harold Macmillan, Churchill's representative in the Mediterranean and later a prime minister himself, clearly understood that Eisenhower possessed some unique qualities that made him the essential Allied rather than American commander: "He has two great qualities which make him easier to deal with than many superficially better-endowed American or British generals. First, he will always listen and try to grasp the point of an argument. Second, he is absolutely fair-minded and, if he has prejudices, never allows them to sway his judgment. Compared to the wooden heads and desiccated hearts of many British soldiers I see here, he is a jewel of broad-mindedness and wisdom."

A glum Eisenhower visits the Tunisia front with Omar Bradley in 1943. Bradley was brought in as Patton's deputy to rejuvenate the leadership of II Corps, but then led II Corps in the final stages of the Tunisia campaign when Patton departed in April to take command of the Seventh US Army for the Sicily landings. (NARA)

In the midst of the Tunisian campaign, Churchill and Roosevelt met again at Casablanca along with Marshall and the other senior British and American commanders. Eisenhower played little role in the conference beyond a brief meeting with Roosevelt. Plans for the 1943 campaigns were thrashed out, with Marshall again pushing for Operation *Roundup* in 1943 and the British again demurring on the grounds that the Allied coalition was still not ready. Churchill pushed for continued operations in the Mediterranean, first against Sicily and then mainland Italy, as a means to knock Italy out of the war and keep the Russians placated.

Operation *Husky* and the Italian tar baby

The British chief of staff Alan Brooke had little confidence in Eisenhower and the US Army after a weak performance in Tunisia. The plans for the Sicily landings, Operation *Husky*, gave the dominant role to Montgomery's Eighth Army while Patton's Seventh US Army was shunted off to a support role. British condescension built up a reservoir of resentment in senior American commanders like Clark, Bradley, and Patton that would later play out in the 1944–45 debates.

Operation *Husky* saw the US Army in Europe come to maturity. A German and Italian counterattack against the US beachhead at Gela was turned back by Patton's Seventh US Army with a professional matter-of-factness. Relations between Patton and Eisenhower began to sour. Egged on by Bradley, Patton increasingly complained about Eisenhower's pro-British bias. Alexander's lingering opinion of the US forces as second rate and not battle worthy colored his planning. Eisenhower was frustrated by Patton's theatrics, and preferred Bradley's calmer and less demanding style. When Montgomery's advance along the eastern coast of Sicily bogged down, Patton exploited Alexander's diffident command style to improvise his own scheme of action with a rapid drive on the provincial capital of Palermo, greatly expanding his force's intended mission. It was a rollicking success and a testament to the capabilities of the US Army under skilled leadership. Patton capped off the venture by racing into Messina ahead of Montgomery's forces, a vindication of improvements in the US Army from earlier in the year.

The success in Sicily encouraged further actions in Italy. Marshall was adamant that US participation in the Mediterranean theater be limited in order to build up forces for Operation *Roundup*. Much to his chagrin, it was painfully evident that the Allies were not ready to conduct *Roundup* in 1943. In the absence of a campaign in northwestern Europe, Churchill continued to advocate continued operations in Italy. The Italian army was wavering and there was a feeling that a good, hard blow would knock Italy out of the war. Under the circumstances, Marshall grudgingly conceded to further operations in Italy, hoping at least that it would tie down German forces that could otherwise be used in France. The Allied joint command had reached maturity by this stage, with Eisenhower remaining in command and only modest organizational changes being carried out.

Starting with Operation *Baytown* on September 3, 1943, Montgomery's Eighth Army crossed the straits of Messina to the tip of the Italian "boot," followed by Operation *Avalanche*,

A conference at Feriana, Tunisia, on March 17, 1943, between Eisenhower, Gen. Harold Alexander, and the newly appointed II Corps commander, Lt. Gen. George S. Patton. (NARA)

an amphibious landing further up the coast at Salerno on September 9, 1943. Operation *Avalanche* did not proceed as well as expected, after being hit by fierce German counterattacks. Clark was in charge of the Fifth US Army, but showed less skill in handling the campaign than was expected in view of his past performance in the Mediterranean. His poisonous relations with Alexander and the British commanders in general did not help matters.

Churchill's depiction of the Mediterranean theater as "the soft underbelly of Europe" was one of his most unfortunate misjudgments. Campaigns in Italy are inevitably dominated by the Italian geography, especially the

Old friends since 1920, Eisenhower and Patton had a tumultuous relationship during the war because of Patton's occasional outbursts. They are seen here at Palermo airport in Sicily on September 17, 1943, after the triumph of Patton's Seventh US Army. (NARA)

Apennine mountain chains that form the spine of the peninsula. Even after the Allies pushed out of Salerno, the narrow coastal plains offered the Allies little room to maneuver. As a result, the fighting in Italy in the autumn and winter of 1943 inevitably involved bitter infantry fighting to overcome determined German defenses in the foothills and mountains. The Allied advance quickly bogged down along the Gustav defensive line in front of Cassino on the western side of the Apennines and in front of Ortona on the eastern side. The obvious solution to this dilemma was an amphibious operation, exploiting the Allies' naval superiority in order to shift forces around the German defenses, as had been done in September 1943 at Salerno. Eisenhower's staff began to look for amphibious opportunities to outflank Rome in October 1943, even as Marshall remained dubious about the American commitment in Italy.

The CCS met again at Quebec in August 1943 to hammer out Allied strategic goals for 1944. Churchill could delay Operation *Roundup* no longer, and a tentative date of May 1944 was set under the new codename of *Overlord*. The Normandy landings would occur in parallel with US Navy amphibious operations in the Pacific against Japan's inner ring of defenses in the Marianas, so amphibious resources would be at a premium. As a result, the Italian theater was drained of troops, with seven divisions shifted

Ike chats with the crew of a British Universal Carrier in Grazziano, Italy, on October 21, 1943, during a tour of the Italian front. (NARA)

to the UK. Future operations in the Italian theater, such as the amphibious landing at Anzio, would have to be accomplished on a shoestring budget. Eisenhower faced the prospect of commanding a peripheral theater, but rumors from Washington suggested that Marshall wanted the *Overlord* command, and in the event Eisenhower would be rotated back to Washington to take over as Army chief of staff.

The Quebec conference moved Allied strategy in the direction of Marshall's plans and away from the dominant role previously played by Churchill and Brooke. This was partly a reflection of growing Allied strength and diminishing German power, which made an invasion of France more feasible, but it was also a recognition of the changing balance of power within the Allied coalition. The British Army was a wasting asset, its reserves of manpower shrinking. It had been a long war for Britain, and overextension of her forces in the colonies meant that the British Army could contribute hardly more than a field army to Normandy, with the slack taken up by the Canadians. The US would start with a commitment of one field army, but this would expand to four by the end of the summer, joined by a French army recreated with American arms.

Eisenhower confers with Lt. Gen. Clark, the commander of Fifth US Army, in Italy on October 22, 1943, a month after Operation *Avalanche*, the amphibious attack at Salerno. (NARA)

Who commands Operation *Overlord*?

The key command issue to be settled in 1943 was the leadership of Supreme Headquarters, Allied Expeditionary Force (SHAEF). Many British leaders assumed it would be a British commander in order to balance Eisenhower's command in the Mediterranean in 1943. Churchill had promised it to Brooke and it was also coveted by his American counterpart, George C. Marshall. Whether he received the post or not, Marshall wanted the SHAEF post in American hands, and had little trouble convincing Roosevelt of this. This had nothing to do with the prestige of the post, but because of Churchill's ambivalent commitment to the *Overlord* invasion planned for 1944. During the Quebec conference, Roosevelt made clear his insistence on an American commander for *Overlord*, and Churchill graciously backed down on his promise to Brooke. This came as a relief to many senior British field commanders. Although few doubted Brooke's merit for the post, he served as a prudent counterweight to Churchill's frequent flights of strategic fancy; Churchill himself recognized this and Brooke remained in London. Eisenhower continued to receive hints in the autumn that he would be relieved of the Mediterranean command and switch places with Marshall; Mediterranean command would switch from Eisenhower to Alexander.

A final decision on who should be SHAEF commander emerged after the "Big Three" conference at Tehran in November 1943 between Churchill, Roosevelt, and Stalin. During the private discussions before the conference,

Adm. King had strongly urged that Eisenhower be nominated since he felt that Marshall could not be spared from Washington. Marshall's interest in the post was no secret and he assured Roosevelt that he would accept either option. Stalin precipitated the final decision by asking who would command *Overlord*. On December 6, 1943, Churchill and Roosevelt visited the Sphinx and Great Pyramid and during the visit the president broached the subject. Roosevelt felt that he could not do without Marshall in Washington, and asked Churchill if Eisenhower would be acceptable. Eisenhower had won Churchill's confidence, and while many senior British commanders still felt that Eisenhower was a lightweight, Churchill agreed to Roosevelt's suggestion. Eisenhower was informed during a visit by the president to Tunis on December 7, 1943. In the two years since the war began, Eisenhower had seen a meteoric rise from a brigadier-general in an obscure staff position to commander of the most powerful armed force in world history.

In late 1943 it appeared that Eisenhower would be transferred back from the Mediterranean theater to take over as Army chief of staff. Here, Ike talks with AAF chief "Hap" Arnold in early December in Sicily. (NARA)

Eisenhower's selection as supreme commander did not complete the command changes. Eisenhower had grown comfortable with the British team in the Mediterranean and promoted Alexander's candidacy for the position of deputy land-forces commander with Churchill. Nevertheless, Eisenhower appreciated that this was largely an internal British decision and did not push the matter too hard. Brooke was not entirely happy with Alexander's laissez-faire command style in Italy and wanted a more forceful commander.

Operation *Husky*: Sicily, July 1943

Eisenhower's Allied Force Headquarters continued to refine amphibious-assault tactics during the 1943 Mediterranean campaign. After having had considerable problems landing tanks during Operation *Torch* in November 1942, the technical solution emerged with the new LST, a US design strongly influenced by the Royal Navy. The Operation *Husky* landings by Patton's Seventh US Army faced some difficult topographical challenges, especially the shallow bay at Gela. The solution is seen here during the unloading of M4A1 medium tanks of the 2nd Armored Division. The LSTs would carry along pontoon causeways on the side of the ships, which would then be disembarked by a SeeBee (US Navy construction battalion: CB) detail. This allowed the LSTs to discharge their cargo from far enough off shore that they had little risk of prematurely running aground. This illustration also shows other innovations developed in the Mediterranean theater. The M4A1 tanks are fitted with a deep-wading kit developed by the Fifth Army Invasion Training Center (5AITC) in Algeria, which allowed the tanks to be unloaded in combat conditions in deeper water and then propel themselves to shore. This would be used under fire for the first time on D-Day in the US Army sector as a more successful alternative than the more fragile DD (Duplex Drive) amphibious tanks.

Eisenhower accompanies President Franklin D. Roosevelt at Castelveltrano airbase in Sicily on December 10, 1943, the day after informing Eisenhower of his assignment as Supreme Commander. Roosevelt made a tour of the Mediterranean theater after the Tehran and Cairo conferences and in the background is Lt. Gen. George S. Patton. (NARA)

Bernard Montgomery was the obvious choice, and on Christmas Eve he was instructed to return to London to take up his new post.

SHAEF

Planning for *Overlord* was a largely British affair under Lieutenant-General Frederick Morgan and his COSSAC (Chief of Staff to the Supreme Allied Command) staff. When Eisenhower arrived in London to take over SHAEF, he in fact wore two distinct hats as both SHAEF Supreme Commander as well as CG ETOUSA. Eisenhower's administrative solution to this was to simplify the command structure by using the existing ETOUSA theater headquarters, merged with Morgan's COSSAC staff, to form the new SHAEF headquarters. The only major element of the ETOUSA headquarters to remain largely autonomous was its logistical arm, the ETO Communications Zone, which was needed to supply and maintain US forces in Europe. Eisenhower continued the "chain" practice from the Mediterranean theater, alternating British and American command positions.

Eisenhower tried to maintain the team that had been created in the Mediterranean. Leadership of the naval side of Operation *Overlord* was in British hands, if for no other reason than the US Navy's single-minded focus on the Pacific theater. Commanding the naval force was Admiral Bertram Ramsay, a happy choice for Eisenhower both because of his professional competence and his connection with the highly admired Adm. Cunningham in the Mediterranean. On the air side, former Fighter Command leader Air Chief Marshal Trafford Leigh-Mallory was in charge of the Allied Expeditionary Air Force (AEAF). Leigh-Mallory was outside the circle of Mediterranean veterans and proved to be an unfortunate choice and the source of endless frustrations for Eisenhower in the months to come. Leigh-Mallory was not adept at dealing with his British counterparts, never mind the Americans. Eisenhower found him to be excessively pessimistic and glum, and the tasks ahead were daunting enough without his constant expressions of doubt about the *Overlord* operation. Fortunately, Eisenhower's deputy supreme commander, Arthur Tedder, had been the air boss in the Mediterranean theater, and would gradually take control of the air side of the command structure.

In spite of their past differences, Eisenhower and Montgomery proved to be an excellent team in improving the *Overlord* plans. Neither Eisenhower nor Montgomery were especially happy with the initial versions of the COSSAC plan, which were based on a weak landing force because of a shortage of amphibious lift. Montgomery took on responsibility for amplifying the D-Day attack from a weak three-division landing to a five-division landing with a more powerful three-division airborne component. It was up to Eisenhower to marshal sufficient LSTs (Landing Ship, Tank) and other critical landing craft to provide *Overlord* with the necessary amphibious lift to permit the expansion of the landing forces. In hindsight it is difficult to recall how precarious the whole enterprise seemed at the time. The Dieppe raid had been an appalling defeat, and both the Salerno landing in September 1943 and the Anzio landing in January 1944 had come close to it. Both Eisenhower and Montgomery were determined to strike so hard on D-Day that the past amphibious misadventures would be forgotten. On landing in France, five Allied divisions would face more than 50 German divisions in France; reinforcement had to come quickly and the Germans had to be prevented from reinforcing the bridgehead, using both battlefield isolation and deception.

Marshall attempted to season the *Overlord* planning by dispatching a Pacific-theater veteran, Lieutenant-General Charles Corlett, to SHAEF. Corlett had commanded the US Army forces during the amphibious landings in the Marshall Islands in February 1944, and was well versed in the new tactical developments in the Pacific, particularly in regards to innovations such as amphibious tractors and naval fire support. He did not arrive until April 1944, and by then Eisenhower's team had little patience to listen to his suggestions with the landings so near. Eisenhower was somewhat insular when dealing with commanders from outside the Mediterranean circle, which also became apparent in his dealings with the former ETOUSA commander, Jacob Devers, who would lead 6th Army Group in southern France later in the summer.

Aside from the challenge of the *Overlord* planning, Eisenhower was soon enmeshed in two major strategic controversies among the Allied senior commanders. The bitterest debate was over the American proposal for simultaneous amphibious landings in France: Operation *Overlord* in Normandy and Operation *Anvil* in southern France. The other controversy revolved around the role of the RAF and AAF strategic bomber forces and Eisenhower's power in controlling their missions.

Through the middle of April 1944, RAF Bomber Command and the AAF's US Strategic Air Force (USSTAF) were committed to the Combined Bomber Offensive under the direction of the RAF's Air Chief Marshal Charles Portal, subordinate to the CCS. The primary mission of the USSTAF was Operation *Pointblank*, the destruction of the Luftwaffe fighter force in preparation for Operation *Overlord*. After April 15, 1944, command

The SHAEF Deputy Supreme Commander was RAF Air Marshal Arthur Tedder. Eisenhower and Tedder made an excellent team as both had established a comfortable working relationship already in the Mediterranean campaign. Tedder's air force experience provided a good balance in the senior command positions, with Eisenhower deferring to Tedder on most of the issues affecting the coalition air forces. (NARA)

The senior Allied commanders are seen in a group portrait at Allied Command HQ in London on February 12, 1944. In the first row are Air Marshal Arthur Tedder, Deputy Supreme Commander; Gen. Dwight Eisenhower, Supreme Commander; and Lt. Gen. Bernard Montgomery, head of ground forces. In the second row are Lt. Gen. Omar Bradley, commander of the First US Army; Adm. Bertram Ramsay, Allied Naval Commander-in-Chief Expedtionary Forces; Air Chief Marshal Trafford Leigh-Mallory, commander Allied Expeditionary Air Forces; and Maj. Gen. Walter Bedell Smith, Eisenhower's deputy. (NARA)

of the heavy-bomber forces was supposed to shift to Leigh-Mallory's AEAF under Eisenhower's SHAEF headquarters. Instead of striking targets deep within Germany, the AEAF wanted to execute the "Transportation Plan," which was aimed at isolating the Normandy battlefield and making it impossible to reinforce by hitting key nodes in the French railroad network, especially marshalling yards. Both Air Marshal Arthur Harris of RAF Bomber Command and Lieutenant-General Carl Spaatz of the USSTAF found Leigh-Mallory to be disagreeable and wanted to have nothing to do with his AEAF headquarters. Nor did they have any confidence in the Transportation Plan, which they felt was a needless diversion of their heavy bombers at a critical time in the air war and a task better suited to the RAF's 2nd Tactical Air Force and the AAF's 9th Air Force.

The Transportation Plan had a broad range of critics, including Churchill who thought that it had the potential to cause massive French civilian casualties. Spaatz in particular was increasingly concerned about the continual diversion of his heavy bombers from their primary missions to secondary political missions, as had been the case in early 1944 when the 15th Air Force based in Italy was being continually taken off the *Pointblank* missions to bomb targets in the Balkans and Romania. Spaatz wanted a transition from the anti-Luftwaffe mission of *Pointblank* to a new "Oil Plan," aimed at crippling the German petroleum industry. The distractions became even worse in April when Churchill began to insist that Spaatz begin to divert heavy bombers to the Operation *Crossbow* mission against German V-1 sites in France; Harris refused to participate in the *Crossbow* campaign, arguing that his night bombers were not accurate enough to attack such small targets. The arguments in March and April 1944 among the senior Army and Air Force commanders became so heated that at various points Tedder, Spaatz, and Eisenhower himself threatened to resign.

In the end, Eisenhower promoted a variety of compromises. He was generally sympathetic to the AAF and saw the bombing campaign against German industry as a historical analog to Sherman's march through Georgia during the Civil War. He understood the air barons' lack of confidence in Leigh-Mallory, and so he reached an agreement with Spaatz to direct the USSTAF through the SHAEF deputy commander, Air Marshal Tedder. Both Tedder and Spaatz had worked together in the Mediterranean theater and had a far more productive relationship. Spaatz reached a compromise with Tedder over the mix of

Above: Eisenhower and Montgomery pay a visit to the 3rd Armored Division during training at Warminster, England, on February 25, 1944; SHAEF deputy commander Arthur Tedder is immediately behind Ike and to the left is Major-General Leroy Watson, the divisional commander. (NARA)

missions, with Tedder finally approving the start of missions against German fuel targets in late April, while at the same time Spaatz used days of bad weather over Germany to conduct *Crossbow* missions over France. In the end, both the Oil Plan and the Transportation Plan had a dramatic impact on the conduct of the Normandy campaign.

The issue of the simultaneous *Anvil* landings in southern France and the *Overlord* landings in Normandy came to a boil in the spring of 1944. The *Anvil* plan was Marshall's scheme to focus Allied attention on the main theater of operations, France, and to suffocate Churchill's misadventures in the Mediterranean, especially Italy. The tactical objective of Operation *Anvil* was to clear the Germans out of southern and central France and to seize Marseilles and neighboring Mediterranean ports in order to provide another logistics stream for Allied forces in France. The CCS agreed at the Tehran conference in November 1943 to limit Italian offensives beyond Rome and instead to focus on a combined *Overlord–Anvil* operation scheduled for May 1944. However, the prospects for *Anvil* dimmed considerably in early 1944. Both Montgomery and Eisenhower agreed that more amphibious landing capability would be need for the Normandy operation, and this absorbed some of the resources planned for *Anvil*. At the same time, Allied operations in Italy had gone badly. The US Army

Below: Churchill and Eisenhower review the 101st Airborne Division on March 23, 1944, with divisional commander Major-General Maxwell Taylor to the right. (NARA)

had reluctantly agreed to an amphibious landing at Anzio in January 1944 as a means to speed up the capture of Rome. Starved of troops and supplies, the Anzio operation soon stalled and turned into a bloody battle of attrition. British planners argued that the Allies could not support three major operations – Italy, *Overlord*, and *Anvil* – simultaneously, and that *Anvil* should be sacrificed. So *Anvil* went into limbo in the spring of 1944, but Marshall and Eisenhower remained committed to its eventual execution.

The other ally: dealing with the French

Of all the diplomatic problems faced by Eisenhower, the most persistent was relations with the French. Eisenhower nearly had his career derailed in the wake of the public scandal in late 1942 after the Darlan–Clark agreement was announced. Admiral Darlan was assassinated on Christmas Eve, 1942, creating a power struggle for dominance of the Free French movement. Général Charles De Gaulle was the self-appointed head of the movement, but the US government did not officially recognize him and he was regarded as an incipient military dictator by the US State Department. De Gaulle's Gouvernement Provisoire de la République Française (GPRF) had no political legitimacy beyond that granted by Britain and the United States. Many factions in the US foreign-policy establishment were pushing for Général Henri Giraud as the recognized head of the Free French forces, but Giraud showed little political aptitude and was outmaneuvered by De Gaulle. Prior to the invasion, the French forces were not represented in SHAEF headquarters except for liaison officers, and they were not informed of the date or location of the *Overlord* landings. The US government did not grant formal recognition to De Gaulle's GRPF until July 13, 1944.

Eisenhower's relations with De Gaulle and the French were more cordial for pragmatic reasons, and Ike was generally ahead of Washington in his relations with the French. He admired the performance of the French troops in the Italian campaign, and recognized that De Gaulle genuinely represented the dreams of the more valiant French to free themselves of the disgrace of the Vichy Regime by their own actions. Eisenhower was not tightly constrained by the State Department's dyspeptic view of De Gaulle, and this freedom of action would play a pivotal role in US decision-making on French affairs in 1944.

Even though Eisenhower held far more favorable views of Free French leader Charles De Gaulle than Roosevelt and the Washington establishment, relations were still quite testy. Here, De Gaulle and Eisenhower confer in Normandy on August 22, 1944, over the issue of the Paris operation. (NARA)

D-Day, June 6, 1944

D-Day was the culmination of a massive joint operation, coordinating naval, air, and land forces. Even an operation as gargantuan and well planned as this was by no means foolproof, and the ultimate challenge in early June was the fickle Channel weather. The landings had narrow windows of time because of the lunar tidal calendar, and the planned landing in the first week of June was dependent on the blustery weather early in the month; if cancelled in June, the next date would be nearly a month later, shortening the summer campaign season. Beginning on June 1, Eisenhower met daily with the senior commanders as well as weather forecasters to decide on when to initiate the great enterprise. Troops boarded their ships in harbors along the English coast, waiting for the "go" signal. A late-evening meeting on June 4 suggested that there might be a 36-hour window of opportunity in the weather; Montgomery was enthusiastic but both Tedder and

Leigh-Mallory were pessimistic. The final decision was Eisenhower's, and he voted "go." A final meeting was held at 0330 on June 5 based on the final weather forecast at 0200 on June 5; Eisenhower reaffirmed the previous evening's decision and the CCS received the coded message: "Halcyon plus 5 and definitely confirmed." The German weather forecast for June 6 suggested: "Invasion possible, but not probable."

Eisenhower spent the evening of June 5, 1944, visiting the paratrooper units preparing for their night mission to Normandy. He remained in England on D-Day, and on June 7 he boarded the minelayer HMS *Aurora* along with Adm. Ramsay to travel to Normandy, where he met with Bradley and the senior US naval commanders. Once ashore, he met with Montgomery to assess the progress of operations. In spite of costly setbacks such as Omaha Beach, the Allies were firmly ashore and moving off the beaches. Eisenhower returned to Portsmouth on June 8, and on June 12 he escorted a delegation of the top US commanders to Normandy on board the destroyer USS *Thompson*, including Marshall, King, and Arnold.

After a spectacular success on D-Day, the June fighting in Normandy proved to be a frustrating month of attritional warfare. The American sector was dominated by bocage, characterized by banked hedgerows and small fields, which proved to be ideal for German defensive purposes by creating a natural structure of fortified barriers. In spite of the difficulties, the US Army gradually adapted and by the end of the month had pushed up the Cotentin peninsula to take the port of Cherbourg on June 27, 1944. The fighting in Montgomery's sector around Caen proved equally difficult, even if the terrain was fundamentally different. The countryside around Caen was mostly open farmland, which was viewed as ideal for the heavily mechanized British force. The Germans recognized the threat in this sector and reinforced it with the available Panzer units, leading to costly tank battles. Instead of being reached on D-Day as had been hoped, Caen did not fall to British troops until July 9, and the breakout from the city was delayed until Operation *Goodwood* on July 18. It was initially expected that the breakout from Normandy was most likely to be in the British sector. Eisenhower's deputy commander, RAF Air Marshal Arthur Tedder, was especially displeased with Montgomery's leadership, and recommended that he be relieved. Eisenhower was not so critical of Montgomery's pace, but there was growing mistrust of his judgment because of Montgomery's tendency to suggest that events were going as planned, and not, as was the case, a necessary change forced by circumstances. By the middle of July, Montgomery was describing the setbacks in the Caen sector as a deliberate attempt from the start to attract the strongest German Panzer forces against his two corps, thereby freeing Bradley to break out in the Saint-Lô sector.

Eisenhower visited with the paratroopers of the 502nd Parachute Infantry, 101st Airborne Division, at Greenham Common airbase on the evening of June 5, 1944, shortly before they took off on their D-Day mission. The two officers behind him are his naval aide, Capt. Harry Butcher, and his British Army aide, Lieutenant-Colonel James Gault. (NARA)

Ike is seen onboard the HMS *Aurora* off Normandy on June 7, conferring with Bradley and the deputy commander of the 9th Air Force, Major-General Ralph Royce. (NARA)

By mid-July the American sector was reinforced as Patton's Third US Army arrived alongside Bradley's First US Army at a point when a breakout finally seemed possible. German forces opposite First US Army had suffered severe attrition and when Operation *Cobra* struck on July 24, 1944, a breakthrough finally occurred. Two armored divisions were ready for exploitation, and once they were injected past Saint-Lô the breakthrough soon turned into a breakout. The role of Patton's Third US Army was to turn westward towards Brittany with the hope of capturing additional port facilities at Quiberon Bay and Brest. Patton's advance was as spectacular as it was fruitless, with the tanks of the 4th and 6th Armored Divisions making 100-mile (160km) dashes in a few days against negligible resistance. This mission had not been adequately reviewed since the experience at Cherbourg in late June, when the Germans had demolished the port. An advance into Brittany served no tactical goal but to seize ports, yet the Germans were likely to demolish them before their capture. Patton raised the issue with Bradley and Eisenhower in early August, eventually leading to a shift in focus.

In the meantime, the collapse of the Saint-Lô front had unhinged German defenses. Hitler reflexively ordered a counterattack, Operation *Lüttich*, aimed at cutting off Patton's spearheads with a race to the sea from

D-Day, Utah Beach, June 6, 1944

D-Day at Normandy was the culmination of Allied combined-arms efforts, leveraging the Allied superiority in naval and air power to land an expeditionary force on a hostile shore. This is an overview of Utah Beach on the far left flank of the Allied landings, an outcome of Eisenhower and Montgomery's scheme to substantially reinforce the original COSSAC Operation *Overlord* plan from three to five divisional sectors. Aside from adding the 4th Division, which landed at Utah, the revised scheme also landed two US airborne divisions behind Utah Beach in order to disrupt any German counterattacks. The landings at Utah Beach occurred with far lower casualties than the other beaches as a result of the airborne disruptions as well as the more effective air support. In contrast to Omaha Beach, where heavy bombers failed to attack the beach defenses, the 9th Tactical Air Force conducted very effective medium-bomber attacks against the Utah Beach defenses, including the missions flown by the B-26B bombers of the 397th Bombardment Group depicted here.

The senior American commanders visited Normandy in June and seen here on June 12, 1944, are AAF chief of staff Henry "Hap" Arnold, Navy chief of staff Adm. Ernie King, Ike, and Army chief of staff George C. Marshall. (NARA)

Mortain towards Avranches. Given the weakened state of the forces in Normandy, the plan was fanciful and had disastrous consequences. Operation *Lüttich* was stopped cold by the US infantry at Mortain, and with Panzer opposition now weakened Montgomery's forces surged forward, creating an enormous pincer around the German 7. Armee at Falaise. The ensuing endgame around Falaise has been the source of endless controversy since August 1944, centering on the argument that Bradley should have pushed his forces into Montgomery's sector to seal the Falaise Gap and trap the remaining German forces. It was by no means clear in August 1944 how many German forces were still in the area, and by the middle of August Bradley had become convinced of Patton's argument that a deep envelopment was possible towards the Seine because of the utter collapse of German defenses. Eisenhower agreed with Bradley's assessment and unleashed Patton in a race towards Paris on August 9.

Eisenhower's next strategic decision was the fate of Paris. Allied planning prior to the Normandy landings presumed that Paris would be avoided as a major objective. The US attitude was bluntly described by Bradley after the war: "Tactically, the city had become meaningless. For all its past glories, Paris represented nothing more than an inkspot on our maps to be bypassed as we headed toward the Rhine. Logistically it could cause untold trouble, for behind its handsome facades there lived 4,000,000 hungry Frenchmen." Bradley's staff had estimated that Paris would require 4,000 tons of supplies per day, which was equivalent to the amount needed to push Patton's Third US Army three days closer towards the German border. Eisenhower saw otherwise. The French resistance began an uprising in the city on August 19, and there was pressure on Eisenhower to liberate the French capital before the Germans could demolish it. Regardless of Bradley's views, the city was the communication hub towards Germany, and it seemed a ripe fruit ready for the picking because of totally inadequate German defensive preparations. Eisenhower could have dawdled and asked Washington's permission to liberate Paris; instead he made a snap decision to intervene in order to prevent needless destruction. The political consequences of allowing Paris to be martyred (as was occurring at the same time to Warsaw) were unthinkable, and Eisenhower authorized the French 2e Division Blindée to race for the city with the support of the US 4th Division. For the US Army, the liberation of Paris was a magnificent conclusion to the bruising summer campaign in Normandy. The ecstatic French crowds in Paris strongly reinforced the popular perception that this was a "good war" worth the bloody sacrifice of Omaha Beach and the grim hedgerow battles in Normandy.

The other D-Day

The prospects for the *Anvil* operation in southern France revived in June 1944 after the Normandy landings and the capture of Rome. A tipping point was the Channel storm on the Normandy coast in late June that wrecked the artificial harbor on Omaha beach. Eisenhower became very concerned about port capacity to supply Allied forces, and the seizure of the ports of Marseilles and Toulon became increasingly attractive. Churchill realized that Operation *Anvil* would strangle his cherished Italian campaign and he made a last-minute plea to Roosevelt, labeling the operation "a major strategic and political error." Marshall and Eisenhower saw *Anvil* as a means to deal with two of the three German field armies in France. Of the two field armies of Heeresgruppe

B, the 7. Armee had been largely eliminated around Falaise or forced into headlong retreat towards the Seine, while the 15. Armee on the Pas-de-Calais had been stripped of its best formations to reinforce Normandy. Heeresgruppe G in central and southern France included the 1. Armee on the Atlantic coast and the 19. Armee in southern France. Operation *Anvil* was intended to rout Heeresgruppe G and so preempt the threat of a prolonged German defense of southern and central France. Based on Marshall's advice, Roosevelt rebuffed Churchill and refused any Balkan adventures. The CCS authorized the landings in southern France on July 14, 1944. The revived plan received a new codename, *Dragoon*, reputedly offered by Churchill, who complained that he had been "dragooned" into the operation.

The landings on the Riviera coast on August 15, 1944, by the Seventh US Army were a spectacular success. The overextended German forces were soon in wholesale retreat towards the Rhine, and Heeresgruppe G had lost half of its forces by late September. The Seventh US Army was soon joined by the French 1ère Armée, under Jacob Devers' 6th Army Group.

Of the three army-group commanders in the ETO, Eisenhower's relations with 6th Army Group commander Jacob Devers were the most distant. Here they are seen at Devers' headquarters on September 4, 1944. (NARA)

The command controversy

August marked another command change in the Allied ranks as the two US field armies were reorganized as the new 12th Army Group under Bradley's command, ending Montgomery's temporary role as overall land-forces commander. In conjunction, Eisenhower moved SHAEF headquarters to the Continent in September, taking overall charge of the land campaign from offices near Versailles outside Paris. Montgomery was never content with this change, and would continue to urge Eisenhower to appoint an overall land-forces commander in the ETO to take over tactical direction, namely himself. Egged on by Brooke, Montgomery pointed to the model of the Mediterranean theater where Alexander had been deputy commander of

European Theater of Operations, June 1944 to May 1945

Labels on map:

Breakout from Rhine bridgeheads, March–April 1945

Advance to the Elbe, April–May 1945

Clearing the National Redoubt, April 1945

German Ardennes offensive, December 1944–January 1945

Over the Vosges, November 1944

Operation *Dragoon*, August–September 1944

Heeresgruppe G retreat, September 1944

Closing on the Rhine, February–March 1945

Westwall battles, October–November 1944

Clearing the Scheldt, October–November 1944

Race to the Seine, August–September 1944

Normandy beachhead, June 1944

Normandy fighting, July 1944

Operation *Cobra* breakout, August 1944

Place names:

Berlin, Plisen, Salzburg, Wismar, Munich, Frankfurt, Zürich, Milano, Rome, Amsterdam, Arnhem, Aachen, Metz, Strasbourg, Antwerp, Paris, London, La Havre, Caen, Cherbourg, Brest, La Rochelle, Royan, Lyon, Marseille, Toulon, Corsica, Sardinia

Bradley — 12

Montgomery — 21

Devers — 6

Seas:

ADRIATIC SEA

MEDITERRANEAN SEA

CELTIC SEA

ATLANTIC OCEAN

Allied monthly advances

- June 6–7, 1944
- June 8–July 7, 1944
- July 8–August 7, 1944
- August 8–September 7, 1944
- September 8–October 7, 1944
- October 8–November 7, 1944
- November 8–December 7, 1944
- February 8–March 7, 1945
- March 8–April 7, 1945
- April 8–May 8, 1945

0   200 miles
0   200km

land forces. Eisenhower retorted that the fundamental difference between the ETO and the Mediterranean was the size of the forces involved: three army groups in the ETO versus only one in the Mediterranean, and that he did not want an unnecessary new layer of command interjected between SHAEF and the three army-group commanders. Eisenhower did not feel that a single ground-forces commander could stay abreast of the developments on all the fronts, and so he preferred a decentralized command structure that gave greater freedom to the three senior Allied army-group commanders.

Eisenhower was issued a 1941 Packard Clipper staff car and he is seen here visiting Bradley's forward headquarters in France on August 12, 1944. Unlike the customized cars operated by Patton and Clark, Eisenhower's car is unadorned beyond the regulation general's plate on the bumper. (NARA)

Although largely unspoken, Eisenhower had serious doubts that Montgomery would have been the ideal choice as the senior tactical commander. Montgomery's star was waning. His leadership in the planning for Operation *Overlord* had been exemplary, but his dissembling about his tactical intentions in the fighting around Caen was troubling. Eisenhower's lingering difficulties with Montgomery were a volatile mixture of policy differences and Montgomery's difficult personality. Montgomery made no secret that he thought Eisenhower's operational vision was fundamentally flawed, and he frequently belittled Eisenhower's tactical judgment. Installing Montgomery in a position of senior command would only aggravate the situation. Not only had he managed to alienate many of the senior US Army commanders in the theater, but most of the senior RAF commanders as well. Eisenhower realized that interjecting Montgomery into a level of command between himself and the army-group commanders would simply add unnecessary friction into the Allied command system. Brooke continued to champion Montgomery and this command solution, which is understandable from a British perspective, but regrettable from an Allied one. Had Brooke and Churchill wanted a British officer as Eisenhower's deputy for land forces, Eisenhower had made it plain before D-Day that he favored Alexander.

Eisenhower was receiving pressure from the American side as well. Behind his back, Patton referred to Eisenhower as "the best general the British have." British hegemony in Allied decision-making was waning as its contribution to the land war diminished. Unlike the original situation in Normandy in June 1944, when Britain contributed the majority of Allied ground forces, by the autumn of 1944 two of the three army groups were American, and this was reflected in tactical air power as well. The balance continued to swing in the American direction because of growing shortages of British infantrymen. Of the 94 Allied divisions under Eisenhower's command in 1945, 62 were American and 11 were French, while Montgomery's army group contained the equivalent of about 21 divisions, including three Canadian divisions and one Polish division.

The decision to eliminate the land-forces-commander post had been planned for many months, and was not based solely on Eisenhower's problems with Montgomery. The Montgomery controversy has obscured other aspects of Eisenhower's efforts to streamline Allied senior command. Not only did the single land-forces-commander position disappear, but Leigh-Mallory's AEAF headquarters was disbanded on October 15, 1944. Coordination of the Allied air forces was centralized under Tedder at SHAEF, but in practice little day-to-day management was necessary as each of the army groups had their own tactical air force for support: the 2nd Tactical Air Force (RAF) with the 21st Army Group, the 9th Air Force with the 12th Army Group, and the 1st Tactical Air Force (Provisional) with the 6th Army Group. Tedder intervened in tactical air issues when joint operations were conducted across the army-group boundaries.

Single thrust or broad front?

By the beginning of September, the Wehrmacht had been routed throughout the depths of France except for a handful of Atlantic ports that Hitler had ordered to be held to the last man. German officers had attempted to assassinate Hitler on July 20, 1944, in the failed "bomb plot." The catastrophe was so deep that German generals later called the period from the end of August to the middle of September "the void." Bradley's and Montgomery's forces raced into Belgium, and by the second week of September they were bumping into the German frontier around Aachen. To many Allied commanders, the collapse of the Wehrmacht before Christmas seemed a real possibility. Instead, the September fighting culminated in two strategic failures and two strategic successes.

Ike and Monty during his visit to Normandy on July 26, 1944, to confer about the Normandy breakout operation. (NARA)

Following the race to the Seine in August, Eisenhower's main operational problem was logistical. The Allied armies had far outpaced their supply trains. On September 11, 1944, the first day US troops entered Germany, the Allies were along a phase line that the Operation *Overlord* plans did not expect to reach until D-Day+330 (May 2, 1945), some 233 days ahead of schedule. Eisenhower had instructed Montgomery to seize the port of Antwerp as a means to solve the logistics problems. British tanks entered Antwerp on September 4, but halted. Although the port was in Allied hands, Montgomery did not push his forces to clear the Scheldt Estuary, without which the port was useless since traffic could be interdicted by German shore batteries. The reasons for this blunder are complex and were caused in part by the excessive optimism of early September that the war would soon be over, in part by Eisenhower's failure to press his commands to Montgomery more forcefully, and finally by Montgomery's focus on a more distant objective: the Rhine.

With the Wehrmacht seemingly on the brink of collapse, Montgomery proposed a bold plan to thrust over the Rhine and put the Allied forces on the brink of the vital Ruhr industrial zone. Three Allied airborne divisions, one British and two American, would lay down an airborne carpet between Allied front lines and the Rhine bridge at Arnhem, clearing the way for a British armored assault along the corridor. Eisenhower was taken aback by the boldness of the plan, as Montgomery was usually a very conservative commander, more prone to excessive preparation than risky gambles. At the same time, Eisenhower had been under some pressure from Marshall to make more imaginative use of the airborne army that the Allies had so painstakingly created and which had been idle since D-Day. Eisenhower, like many of the other senior Allied commanders, was caught up in the euphoria of the race over the Seine, and approved Montgomery's plan for Operation *Market Garden*.

The operation was indirectly doomed by one of the Allies' successes. Spaatz's "Oil Plan" had succeeded beyond his wildest imagination. The bombing missions had hit at Germany's Achilles heel, the synthetic-fuel plants that were the source of all the Luftwaffe's aviation fuel. The massive loss of fuel in the attacks, as well as the destruction of production facilities, exhausted much of the German stocks of aviation fuel by September, grounding much of the Luftwaffe except for the fighter force. The loss of the Romanian oil fields to the Red Army's summer offensive only deepened the crisis, and cut both the Army's and Kriegsmarine's fuel reserves. The German Army received priority for remaining fuel supplies, and the Kreigsmarine was forced to leave most of its warships in harbor, with the exception of small numbers of U-boats. As a result of the fuel shortages there were large numbers of idle Luftwaffe and Kriegsmarine troops at precisely the time that the Army badly needed replacements. These troops were hastily dispatched to the west to help recreate shattered German divisions. By the middle of September, the Wehrmacht had already reached its nadir and was beginning to recover its ferocious defensive potential; German morale revived once the fighting reached German soil. This abrupt change was later dubbed the "Miracle on the Westwall" ("*Wunder am Westwall*"). Although this change is evident in historical retrospect, it was certainly not clear in early September 1944, and Allied planners expected to see the German Army collapse much as it had done in November 1918.

As a result, the *Market Garden* gamble failed in the face of the sudden Wehrmacht revival. The British 1st Airborne Division did reach and hold the bridge at Arnhem, but the relieving tank columns were never

Three future Army chiefs of staff confer on July 5, 1944, in Normandy. To Eisenhower's right are Lt. Gen. Omar Bradley, at the time First US Army commander, and Major-General Lawton "Lightning Joe" Collins, commander of VII Corps, which was responsible for the liberation of the port of Cherbourg at the end of June and which spearheaded Operation *Cobra* later in July 1944. (NARA)

able to reach them. The narrow corridor to Arnhem was soon the scene of fierce German counterattacks. While Montgomery and Eisenhower were focused on "the bridge too far," the German 15. Armee was methodically reinforcing its defenses along the Scheldt Estuary, fully appreciating that without control of the waterway the port of Antwerp was useless. It would take nearly three more months of fighting before the Scheldt was cleared and the port opened.

An important Allied strategic success in September 1944 was the establishment of a solid Allied front from the North Sea to the Mediterranean with the advance of Devers' 6th Army Group from the Riviera to the Vosges Mountains. Patton's Third US Army began to meet elements of the French 1ère Armée around Autun on September 10, and pockets of trapped German troops continued to surrender through the middle of the month. The precipitous retreat of Heeresgruppe G from southern and central France led to the loss of about 200,000 troops. This marked the liberation of nearly all of France. Without Operation *Dragoon*, the Wehrmacht would have held the majority of France, with Allied control of only the northeastern region. This would have allowed the Wehrmacht to continue to conduct counteroffensives along a broad front and to tie down Allied forces either along a defensive perimeter in France and in operations to clear the rest of the country.

By the end of September Eisenhower could look back at the tremendous Allied achievement with the success of *Overlord* and the Normandy breakout, while at the same time the dream of an end to the war by Christmas had evaporated. SHAEF planning for the defeat of Germany intended to "rapidly starve Germany of the means to continue the war" with an emphasis on the capture of the two industrial concentrations in western Germany: the Ruhr and the Saar Basin. Of the two regions, the Ruhr was the more significant, and the loss of the Ruhr combined with the loss of the Low Countries would eliminate 65 percent of German steel production and 56 percent of its coal production. Besides the ground campaign, SHAEF supervised the destruction of German industry by expanded Allied bomber attack.

Allied strategic planning had focused on two principal invasion routes into Germany: the Aachen–Stolberg corridor towards Westphalia on the northern side of the Ruhr, and the Moselle gate in the Saar towards central Germany. These choices were reflected in German defenses as well, as can be seen from the layout of the Westwall, with both these sectors being the most heavily fortified. Even after the *Market Garden* failure, Montgomery and Brooke pushed for a single northern thrust by the 21st Army Group, while Eisenhower preferred a broad-front approach, albeit one favoring the northern wing. Eisenhower's viewpoint had been previously explained in a May 18, 1944 report on "Post-Overlord Planning" by the SHAEF Staff: 'The Allies should advance on more than one axis of advance to keep the Germans guessing as to the direction of our main thrust, cause them to extend their forces, and lay the German forces open to defeat in detail.

Alternate plans, August 1944

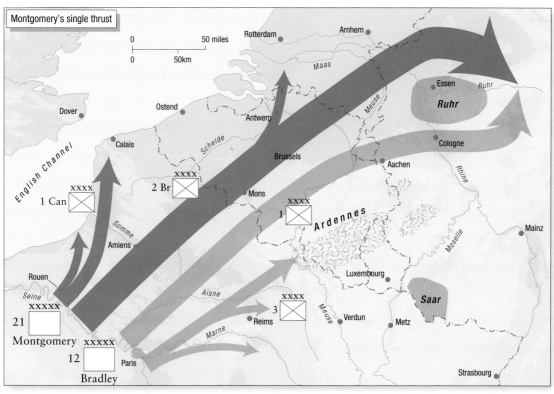

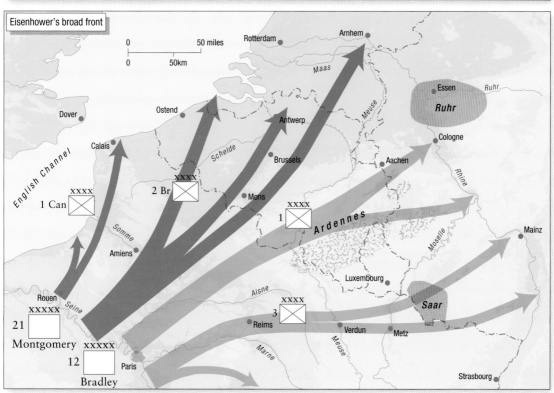

A single axis would lead us to collisions with the enemy main forces on narrow fronts and with no power of maneuver or surprise.'

The debate about a broad versus a narrow front was temporarily submerged after the failure of Operation *Market Garden*. The shortfall in Allied logistics left Eisenhower with two broad strategic tempos for the autumn campaign. One of Eisenhower's options was to temporarily cease operations along the German frontier until the logistics could catch up; this was the option chosen by the Red Army, which had halted operations on its Central Front in Poland after August 1944 in order to build up strength for the final offensive into Germany in the early winter of 1945. Eisenhower was not keen on this option as it would permit the Germans to rebuild the Wehrmacht in relative peace and result in a more formidable opponent when the offensive resumed in early 1945 after the winter weather abated. Instead, Eisenhower decided to conduct limited offensive operations that would drain the Wehrmacht by attrition. Some senior US commanders, such as Bradley, believed that it might be possible to reach the Rhine in the autumn, a viewpoint that gradually succumbed to reality in the face of determined German defenses. The resulting fighting was a frustrating and costly battle of attrition. From October 1 to December 16, the Germans lost about 350,000 casualties and prisoners, but Allied territorial gains were modest and casualties high.

A bloody slog: the autumn 1944 campaigns

In Montgomery's 21st Army Group sector, Eisenhower finally insisted that the Scheldt Estuary be cleared, and the port of Antwerp was finally opened to traffic by the end of November 1944. In the center, Bradley's 12th Army Group was split by the Ardennes, with the Ninth and First US Armies fighting in the Aachen–Stolberg corridor, largely disconnected from Patton's Third US Army and its actions in the Metz area. These distinct campaigns had mixed results. The First US Army became bogged down trying to clear the Hürtgen Forest, an effort connected to a belated recognition that the

Roer River dams needed to be breached or captured before the 12th Army Group could maneuver over the Roer flood plains towards the Rhine. To end the stalemate, Bradley hoped that Operation *Queen* in mid-November would enable the First US Army to finally break out of the Aachen–Stolberg region. This offensive was frustrated by the weather, terrain, and stiff German defenses. Patton's attack against the Metz fortress complex finally succeeded in late 1944, and this pushed the Third US Army up against the formidable Westwall defenses in the Saar.

The most successful of the three Allied army groups in the autumn was Devers' often-ignored 6th Army Group, which was assigned the daunting task of reaching the Rhine plains around Strasbourg over the Vosges Mountains. The Vosges had not been conquered in modern times, but the Italian-front veterans of the Seventh US Army and French 1ère Armée penetrated the Vosges passes and the Belfort Gap in November. This was the first Allied army group to achieve a firm foothold on the Rhine, reaching the river on November 19 and seizing the Alsatian capital of Strasbourg in a bold tank attack on November 23. Devers wanted to cross the Rhine in December and advance northward, undermining the German defenses in the Saar facing Patton's Third US Army. But Eisenhower was not convinced that the 6th Army Group had the capabilities to conduct operations on the eastern bank of the Rhine in the Black Forest area, and instead instructed Devers to support Patton's planned December 19 offensive towards Frankfurt, Operation *Tink*, by driving northward through the Hagenau Gap into the Saar-Palatinate.

By early December 1944, with Antwerp open and the supply situation improving, Eisenhower began to refine plans for the 1945 offensive operations. Instead, the Germans struck first with their Ardennes offensive on December 16, 1944, thereby diverting Allied intentions for more than a month. The early successes of the German Ardennes offensive were because of a major Allied intelligence failure. Eisenhower and his subordinate commanders had become so accustomed to the value of the Ultra signals intelligence bonanzas that they undervalued the continuing need for more traditional means of intelligence assessment. There was a tendency to mirror-image German intentions and to assume that the German buildup in the Eifel was a preparatory action by the Wehrmacht to create a counterattack force to deal with the anticipated Allied lunge for the Rhine in January–February 1945. Hitler was far more desperate than Eisenhower or Bradley imagined, and far more ready to take foolhardy risks.

Although the German attack caught Eisenhower and Bradley off guard, their instinctive belief that the Ardennes provided a poor tactical avenue in the winter months proved essentially correct. Eisenhower was able to mobilize SHAEF's prodigious infrastructure to rapidly move reinforcements into the Ardennes, while at the same time Tedder directed the Allied air forces on a campaign to isolate the battlefield, first by bombing German marshalling yards in the Eifel and then, once the weather cleared, to conduct tactical interdiction with fighters and light bombers. The German attack was halted before Christmas far from its main objective of Antwerp, and the next three weeks saw a bloody battle of attrition as the bulge was reduced.

Ike's decision to pursue a strategy of attrition in the autumn of 1944 had a high human cost, nowhere more evident than in the savage fighting in the Hürtgen Forest. He is seen here talking with Major-General Norman Cota, who was in command of the 28th Division at the time. After suffering staggering casualties, the division was sent to the Ardennes to recuperate, only to be smashed again during the German offensive on the approaches to Bastogne. (NARA)

Autumn frustrations, September 15 to December 15, 1944

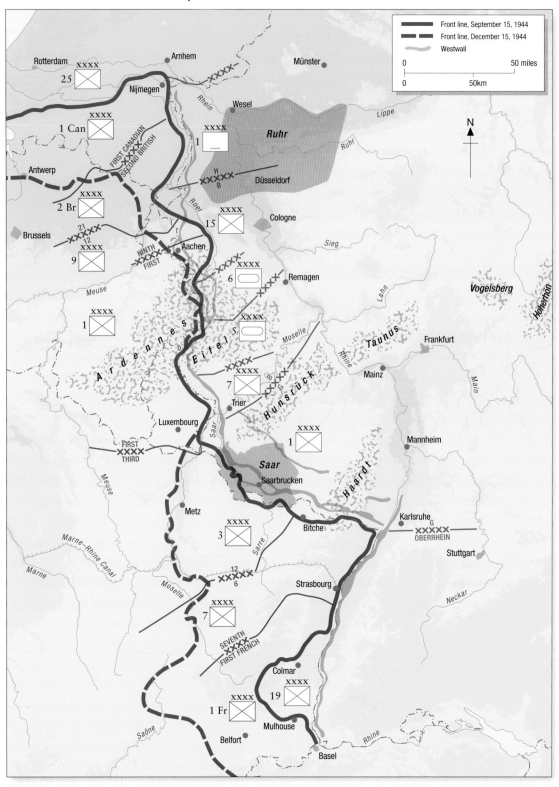

Front line, September 15, 1944
Front line, December 15, 1944
Westwall

0   50 miles
0   50km

N

From an operational perspective, Eisenhower's response after Christmas was prudent but cautious, with the exception of Patton's dynamic relief of Bastogne. Bradley and Eisenhower suffered a blow to their confidence by failing to anticipate the German offensive. Control of the northern wing of the Ardennes front was temporarily handed over to Montgomery, which helped to tidy up the sector but aggravated the growing antagonism between Bradley and Montgomery. The US Army's defeat of the German Army in the Ardennes crippled the Wehrmacht in the west and facilitated the offensive operations into northwestern Germany in February and March 1945.

The calm before the storm. Eisenhower and Bradley meet with VIII Corps commander Troy Middleton in Wiltz, Luxembourg, on November 5, 1944. Middleton's corps was assigned to take over the "ghost front" in the Ardennes, where little combat was expected. (NARA)

In contrast to the Ardennes, the Seventh US Army in Alsace caught wind of the subsidiary German offensive, Operation *Nordwind*, by more careful use of traditional intelligence techniques. This proved to be vital, since their front had been grossly overextended in order to cover the sector that Patton had vacated when two of his corps were dispatched towards Bastogne. When the German attacks began in the early morning hours of New Year's Day 1945, they were stopped in a few days' fighting. Eisenhower had ordered Devers to pull the Seventh US Army back into the Vosges until the more important Ardennes sector was cleared, but Devers dragged his heels, feeling that his forces were better positioned for defense along the trace of the Maginot line than back in the mountains. The debate turned into a political maelstrom, since any pullback would involve the abandonment of Strasbourg, which was completely unacceptable to the Free French. Preoccupied with the larger crisis in the Ardennes, Eisenhower underestimated the consequence of his hasty orders, and Churchill volunteered to mediate the dispute between Ike and De Gaulle. By the time the controversy reached its head on January 3, both the Alsace and Ardennes fronts had stabilized and Eisenhower backed off from his instructions to abandon Strasbourg.

The Battle of the Bulge precipitated another crisis in Allied command, after Montgomery made a number of tactless remarks to the press that exaggerated his own role in the victory. Eisenhower was fed up, and began steps to relieve Montgomery. Wishing to avoid a public row, Eisenhower first informed Monty's chief of staff, Major-General Francis de Guingand. On learning of Ike's intentions, Montgomery backed down. This incident largely ended Montgomery's attempts to maneuver himself into command of land forces in the ETO.

Congratulations are in order for Patton in February 1945 after the splendid performance of his Third US Army in the relief of Bastogne during the Battle of the Bulge. Eisenhower is seen here with Bradley and Patton on February 5, 1945, in Bastogne. (NARA)

To the Rhine

Following the Battle of the Bulge at the end of January 1945, Eisenhower intended to conduct a three-phase operation to trap and destroy as much of the German Army as possible on the west bank of the Rhine prior to major river-crossing operations. The first phase of the plan was to close on the Rhine north of Dusseldorf in anticipation of Operation *Plunder*, the main Rhine crossing in Montgomery's 21st Army Group sector. The second phase was to close on the Rhine from south of Dusseldorf, in anticipation of a secondary operation by Devers' 6th Army Group on the Upper Rhine. The third phase would be the advance into the plains of northern Germany and into central-southern Germany along with Bradley's 12th Army Group once the Rhine was breached. Eisenhower's plans were again contested by Montgomery and the British Chiefs of Staff, who continued to favor a single thrust by Montgomery's 21st Army Group reinforced with US corps, with Berlin as its objective. Eisenhower repeated his opposition to this approach, judging that a single thrust offered the Germans an opportunity to concentrate their dwindling resources. Even if Eisenhower had decided on a single bold thrust to Berlin, it is doubtful whether Montgomery would have been his choice to conduct such an operation given his cautious and methodical tactical style. During the debate over the Rhine plans, Eisenhower was taken aside by Marshall and assured that his plans would be accepted by the CCS regardless of the complaints by the British Chiefs of Staff. Nevertheless, in deference to Brooke and Montgomery, Eisenhower's plan continued to lean towards a northern focus in the final assault into Germany.

The first phase of the Allied offensive began on 8 February with two operations aimed at closing on the Rhine in the northern sector. Operation *Veritable* was Montgomery's effort to push the 21st Army Group through the Reichswald to the west bank of the Rhine prior to Operation *Plunder*. Operation *Grenade* was a supporting effort by the Ninth US Army to finally clear the Roer River, and especially the river's dams, as a prelude to future operations along the Rhine. Operation *Veritable* proved more difficult than anticipated because of the flooded terrain and stubborn German resistance, but the Ninth US Army reached the Rhine on March 2, followed by the First Canadian Army. The Ninth US Army proposed to use nine of its 12 divisions to conduct a surprise crossing of the Rhine, but Montgomery preferred to wait for Operation *Plunder* later in the month.

The land campaign was supported by a major air initiative, Operation *Clarion*. This was a massive single-day strike by 9,000 Allied aircraft, directed against the German railroad network. Hopes that this would lead to a complete collapse of the German railway system were disappointed, and *Clarion* added simply one more burden on an already debilitated Wehrmacht.

Clarion was followed in March by Operation *Bugle*, a more focused attempt to isolate the Ruhr by cutting critical bridges, viaducts, and rail links in order to isolate its industry and weaken its defenses against the upcoming Allied ground onslaught.

With the initial phase of the Allied offensive complete, Operation *Lumberjack* began on March 1, 1945, with the First US Army clearing the west bank of the Rhine from the Cologne area south, linking up with Patton's Third US Army on the Ahr River near Koblenz. On March 7, the 9th Armored Division discovered that the Ludendorff Bridge over the Rhine had not been demolished like all the other major Rhine bridges, and quickly captured it, to everyone's surprise.

This sudden windfall called for another reconsideration of operations into Germany. Bradley proposed a new scheme, Operation *Voyage*, which aimed at linking up the First and Third US Armies on the eastern bank of the Rhine and then driving to the northeast to create a southern pincer around the Ruhr to complement Montgomery's attack from the north. While Eisenhower would not immediately initiate Operation *Voyage*, Bradley's proposal further undermined his commitment to Montgomery's northern thrust. When Montgomery again pressed him with an extravagant demand for another ten US divisions for the already elephantine Operation *Plunder*, Eisenhower outmaneuvered him by offering the additional units on the condition that Bradley's 12th Army Group be given back control of all the First and Ninth US Army units scheduled to participate in Operation *Plunder*. With his bluff called, Montgomery backed off, preferring to have only the Ninth US Army under his control than to have double the US reinforcements but all under Bradley's command.

In the meantime, Devers' 6th Army Group had already initiated Operation *Undertone*, an attack up the west bank of the Rhine to undermine German defenses in front of Patton's Third US Army. This succeeded more quickly than expected, and Patton launched his attack into the Saar-Palatinate, which collapsed the German defenses so quickly that it was dubbed the "Rhine rat race." With Montgomery's Operation *Plunder* scheduled to begin on March 24, Patton made it a point to put a division across the Rhine at Oppenheim on the night of March 22–23, teasing his former rival with a boast that his army had managed to cross the Rhine without artillery or any other heavy support.

With the German defenses along the Rhine on the verge of a rout, Montgomery finally staged his *Plunder* extravaganza near Wesel on March 24, and Eisenhower gave Bradley permission to explode out

This senior command meeting at Third US Army headquarters near Gotha on April 12, 1945, started out on a happy note with the generals posing in front of a captured German Bf-100 heavy fighter. The meeting turned grim later in the day when Eisenhower and the other generals first visited one of the newly discovered concentration camps nearby. Seen here from left to right are Troy Middleton (VIII Corps), Walton Walker (XX Corps), James Van Fleet (III Corps), George Patton (Third US Army), Eisenhower, and Omar Bradley (12th Army Group). (NARA)

Crossing the Rhine

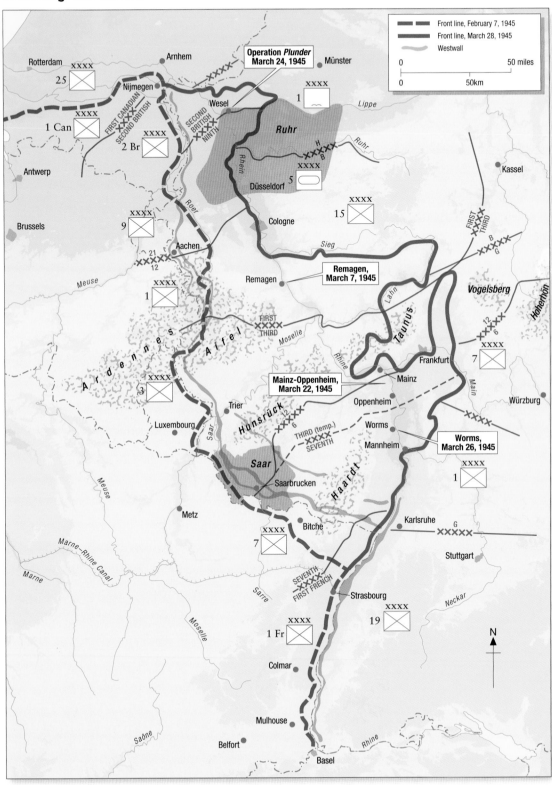

	Front line, February 7, 1945
	Front line, March 28, 1945
	Westwall

0 _____ 50 miles
0 _____ 50km

Operation *Plunder*
March 24, 1945

Remagen,
March 7, 1945

Mainz-Oppenheim,
March 22, 1945

Worms,
March 26, 1945

Rotterdam · Arnhem · Münster · Wesel · Nijmegen · Antwerp · Brussels · Aachen · Cologne · Remagen · Kassel · Düsseldorf · Frankfurt · Würzburg · Mainz · Oppenheim · Worms · Mannheim · Trier · Luxembourg · Saarbrucken · Metz · Bitche · Karlsruhe · Stuttgart · Strasbourg · Colmar · Mulhouse · Belfort · Basel

Ruhr · Lippe · Rhein · Ruhr · Sieg · Lahn · Taunus · Vogelsberg · Hohertön · Moselle · Rhine · Main · Neckar · Ardennes · Aifel · Hunsrück · Saar · Haardt · Meuse · Saar · Sarre · Moselle · Marne–Rhine Canal · Marne · Saône · Rhine

25 · 1 Can · 2 Br · 9 · 1 · 3 · 7 · 1 Fr · 19 · 1 · 5 · 15 · 7 · H B · G B

FIRST CANADIAN
SECOND BRITISH
SECOND BRITISH NINTH
FIRST THIRD
FIRST THIRD
THIRD (temp.) SEVENTH
SEVENTH FIRST FRENCH

21 12

N

of the Remagen bridgehead with Operation *Voyage* on March 25. Operation *Voyage*, and the slow progress of Montgomery's forces out of the Wesel bridgehead, prompted Eisenhower to reorient the focus of Allied operations into Germany to a central rather than a northern emphasis. Lieutenant-General Simpson's Ninth US Army was taken from Montgomery's control and returned to Bradley in late March, which led to another spate of arguments with Brooke and Montgomery. One of Eisenhower's principal aims since D-Day had been to avoid alienating the senior British commanders; with the war nearly won he finally ignored this rule in favor of ending the war as quickly as possible by placing greater reliance on the US field armies.

The following weeks' fighting saw the collapse of the Wehrmacht in the west. On April 1 the Ruhr pocket was encircled by elements of the Ninth US Army from the north and the First US Army from the south; the pocket held out until April 18, but within it was most of Heeresgruppe B and 317,000 German troops, the largest German surrender of the war. The new Fifteenth US Army was added to the Allied order of battle and was assigned to clean up the Ruhr pocket while the other formations advanced eastward.

Endgame in Europe

In mid-March, German armaments minister Albert Speer reported to Hitler that in the wake of Allied air attacks on the German rail network and industy, "The final collapse of the German economy can therefore be counted on with certainty within four to eight weeks... After this collapse, even military continuation of the war will become impossible." The two principal Allied operational debates in the spring of 1945 were the capture of Berlin and the threat of the "National Redoubt." The final month of combat in the ETO was heavily shaped by agreements made between Stalin, Churchill, and Roosevelt in their conferences. A scheme for the occupation of Germany had been finalized at Yalta in February 1945, defining the sectors that would be held by the Allied armies.

Prior to Yalta, Eisenhower had seen two principal objectives in Germany: the industrial heart of the Ruhr, and the political heart of Berlin. Although Allied planning had long assumed that Berlin was "the main prize," after Yalta, Eisenhower backed away from this viewpoint. Berlin had been assigned to the Soviet occupation zone, and Eisenhower was unwilling to risk the heavy casualties likely in this final battle only to have to withdraw back to the Elbe. Bradley ventured that a Berlin attack would cost 100,000 casualties, which Eisenhower judged "a pretty stiff price for a prestige objective." In addition, the Red Army was closer to Berlin and far more likely to reach the city first. By late March 1945 the Red Army was on the Oder River, with lead elements within 30–40 miles (50–65km) of the German capital; Montgomery's 21st

The first steps towards desegregation of the US Army took place under Eisenhower's instructions in January 1945 when he authorized volunteer African-American troops to join previously segregated infantry divisions. Aside from a small number of segregated combat battalions, most African-American troops in the ETO served in combat-support units, and here Ike talks to Private Edward Clay at a First US Army fuel dump in November 1944. (NARA)

Army Group was more than 200 miles (320km) away. If British or American forces reached the western side of Berlin concurrently with the Red Army on the eastern side, coordination of a joint campaign would have been a nightmare. Actual Soviet casualties in the Berlin operation were 352,000, including 78,000 killed.

On March 28 Eisenhower sent instructions to the Allied military missions in Moscow to inform the Red Army of his operational intentions, in the hope of clarifying the junction of Anglo-American and Soviet forces in the upcoming months. The message was delivered to the Soviet government on the night of March 31 and indicated that once German forces in the Ruhr had been encircled and destroyed, the main thrust would be towards Erfurt, Leipzig, and Dresden; a secondary thrust would be made as soon as possible in the Regensburg–Linz area to prevent the formation of a National Redoubt. Berlin was specifically excluded as an objective. Eisenhower's letter caused a furor from Brooke and the British Chiefs of Staff, who accused him of overstepping his authority. Marshall and the Joint Chiefs of Staff offered an equally blistering response to Brooke that Eisenhower was the only commander in a position to judge what measures were best for destroying the German forces and their will to resist, as well as the need to coordinate joint operations with the Red Army. The arguments became so heated that both Churchill and Roosevelt were obliged to intervene. Eisenhower made a presentation of his views to the CCS on April 7, 1945, in which he concluded

Eisenhower's most controversial decision in 1945 involved the choice of whether or not to try to capture Berlin. Here, Eisenhower and Soviet Marshal Georgi Zhukov, the victor of Berlin, watch an air demonstration during Zhukov's visit to SHAEF headquarters in Frankfurt in July 1945. (NARA)

The Battle of the Bulge, December 19, 1944

Following the surprise German offensive in the Ardennes on December 16, 1944, Eisenhower ordered his senior commanders to meet on December 19 in Verdun to discuss the Allied counterattack. The meeting was held in a vacated schoolroom in a complex of buildings assigned to the 12th Army Group since October 1944. Bradley had not used the complex, preferring a forward headquarters in Spa, Belgium, and this site was chosen since it was away from the threatened area and between Eisenhower's Versailles headquarters, Patton's headquarters in Etain, and Bradley's Belgian headquarters. Present at the meeting were Ike, Bradley, Patton, Devers, Tedder, Smith, and Freddie de Guingand representing Montgomery. The initial briefing was given by Ike's G-2 (intelligence officer), Major-General Kenneth Strong. It was at this meeting that Patton unveiled his scheme to relieve Bastogne. Two of his corps had been mobilized to launch Operation *Tink* towards Frankfurt that same day, and instead he proposed to wheel them northward instead of eastward. Patton's bravura performance that day helped seal his legend as the most aggressive US field-army commander of the war. Seen here are Bradley (**1**), Patton (**2**), and Devers (**3**) as Eisenhower (**4**) studies one of Strong's intelligence maps.

that "if the Combined Chiefs of Staff should decide that the Allied effort to take Berlin outweighs the purely military considerations in this theater, I would cheerfully readjust my plans and my thinking so as to carry out such an operation." The CCS declined to do so, leaving the conduct of the final operations up to Eisenhower.

The ultimate dividing line with the Red Army in April was the Elbe River. The first of the Western Allied forces to approach Berlin was Simpson's Ninth US Army, which first reached the river on April 12 near Tangermunde, 53 miles (85km) from Berlin. On April 15 Simpson conferred with Bradley about making a thrust for Berlin, but Eisenhower instructed them to consolidate their positions and wait for the Red Army.

Eisenhower's intention for Montgomery's 21st Army Group was for it to advance into Denmark in order to cordon this area off from Soviet advances. The First Canadian Army completed the liberation of the Netherlands in early April, and then the 21st Army Group proceeded to the northeast towards the North Sea coast in the latter half of April. After pushing into Holstein in late April and early May, the 21st Army Group advanced as far as the Kiel Canal, sealing off Denmark, and then to the Baltic near Wismar, where Soviet troops were first met on May 2, 1945.

By the third week of April, Eisenhower and the Soviet chief of staff, General Alexei Antonov, had agreed to use the Mulde River as the boundary for the southern junction of Allied forces. The first junction of Allied forces was made near Torgau on April 25, 1945.

One of the more curious aspects of Eisenhower's final plans was the frequent mention of the National Redoubt as a secondary operational objective. By mid-March 1945, SHAEF was convinced that a significant threat existed of prolonged German resistance in the Bavarian Alps even after the German main forces had been defeated. As a result, Devers 6th Army Group and elements of Patton's Third US Army were directed southeastward in the last two weeks of April 1945 to clear out any potential resistance centers. In fact there was no scheme for a National Redoubt, but the effort pushed Allied forces into northwest Austria near Obersalzburg and Linz, and across the Czechoslovak border.

Patton's advance southeastward out of Bayreuth raised the issue of whether Allied forces should attempt to liberate Prague. Brooke and the British Chiefs of Staff pushed this option, but Eisenhower remained skeptical. On May 4, Eisenhower consulted with Antonov about moving deeper into Czechoslovakia, but the Russians asked him to maintain a line along the towns of Karlsbad, Pilsen, and Ceske Budejovice,

Eisenhower and the senior American ETO commanders pose for a group portrait on May 11, 1945. The first row from left to right are William Simpson (Ninth US Army), George Patton (Third US Army), Carl Spaatz (USSTAF), Eisenhower, Omar Bradley (12th Army Group), Courtney Hodges (First US Army), and Leonard Gerow (Fifteenth US Army). The upper row from left to right are Ralph Stearley (XIX Tactical Air Command), Hoyt Vandenberg (9th Air Force), Walter Smith (SHAEF chief of staff), Otto Weyland (XIX Tactical Air Command), and Richard Nugent (XXIX Tactical Air Command). (NARA)

and pointed out that they viewed this is a reciprocal gesture for SHAEF's request that the Red Army stay east of Wismar and out of Denmark. As a result, Patton halted his forces on the Moldau River, even after the Czechs staged an uprising in Prague on May 5. With nearly all of Germany overrun and Hitler dead, the remnants of the German government sued for peace.

OPPOSING COMMANDERS

Eisenhower's nearest counterpart during World War II was Albert Kesselring, who commanded German forces in the Mediterranean theater at the time of the Tunisian campaign and the early Italian campaign. Curiously enough, Kesselring was also one of Eisenhower's opponents in the final month of the war. Kesselring, like Eisenhower, had his share of problems as a joint commander with his Italian counterparts.

Kesselring had begun his military career in the Bavarian artillery, being elevated to the general staff in the winter of 1917 as a result of his demonstrated talent. He remained in the Reichswehr and in 1933 he was ordered to become chief administrator of the Air Ministry in civilian mufti. His primary responsibility was the creation of the infrastructure of the new Luftwaffe, and he attracted the favorable attention of the Luftwaffe head, Hermann Göring. By the time war broke out he had returned to uniform as commander of Luftflotte 1, the tactical close-support bomber and Stuka force that played a prominent role in the 1939 campaign against Poland, and later as commander of Luftflotte 2 during the 1940 campaign against France. When German forces expanded their presence in the Mediterranean, the Wehrmacht established Oberbefelshaber Süd (Commander-in-Chief South) at Frascati near Rome, with Generalfeldmarschall Albert Kesselring taking command in December 1941. In addition to his role as Oberbefelshaber Süd, he commanded Luftflotte 2, the Luftwaffe force covering the Mediterranean. Kesselring was nominally under the command of Mussolini himself, and served as the air commander to the Italian Comando Supremo (High Command). Kesselring's command relationship with the Italians and with Rommel was awkward, and depended on his considerable political skills. Marshal Ugo Cavalerro was the chief of the Italian Comando Supremo and he took Kesselring's appointment as a personal slight. As a result, German–Italian high-command relations were strained from the outset and became even worse in February 1943 when Cavalerro was replaced by Generale Vittorio Ambrosio, who exhibited "an unfriendly, even hostile attitude" according to Kesselring. Kesselring's official title changed on November 21, 1943, to Oberbefelshaber Südwest (Commander-in-Chief Southwest) after the

Eisenhower's opponent in the Mediterranean theater was Luftwaffe Generalfeldmarschall Albert Kesselring, one of Germany's most skilled field commanders. (NARA)

Italians signed an armistice with the Allies. His political charms led to his nickname "Smiling Albert," a curious parallel to Eisenhower's well-known grin. In 1943 Kesselring had tactical authority over all German military units in Italy, including the Luftwaffe and Kriegsmarine, though commanders in Italy nominally reported to their service commanders in Berlin.

Kesselring was an unusual figure in such a command post, as he was a Luftwaffe officer, not an Army officer. His varied career and organizational talents made him an ideal theater commander, able to deal with both the Luftwaffe and the Army. Kesselring carried out his tasks with considerable skill, managing to keep the Italians mollified while keeping some of the more rambunctious German commanders such as Erwin Rommel in check. In spite of his lack of experience in divisional or corps commands, he proved to be an astute and effective operational leader and certainly one of Germany's most talented commanders during the war.

Kesselring proved more adept in the Mediterranean in 1943 than Eisenhower. He recognized early on the threat that the *Torch* landings posed to Rommel and rapidly reinforced the Tunisian bridgehead. It was largely through his foresight, by reinforcing the units in Sicily and in Tunisia itself, that the Luftwaffe was able to maintain a measure of air superiority over Tunisia in early 1943. Kesselring's defense planning for Sicily was effective in spite of the wavering support of the Italian Army, which by this stage of the war was largely defeatist. Under his direction, the evacuation of German forces over the Messina Straits at the end of the Sicily campaign played a central role in Germany's ability to defend the rest of Italy through 1943. Kesselring took superb advantage of Italy's defensive potential, and his superior performance encouraged Hitler to take a hands-off approach in the Italian theater compared to others. Instead of Hitler's preference for last-ditch "defense to the death," Kesselring preferred to defend as long as possible, create new defense lines in the rear, and retreat in a coherent fashion at an opportune moment. Italy became a costly stalemate for both sides, largely because of Kesselring's excellent leadership and his skillful use of modest resources. When Kesselring faced Eisenhower again in the final month of the war, the outcome was preordained no matter how good his leadership skills were.

Eisenhower had no true counterparts during the 1944-45 campaign in the ETO, because of the fundamental difference in organization between the Allies and the Wehrmacht. A unified German command nominally rested in the hands of the Oberkommando der Wehrmacht (OKW), headed by Generalfeldmarshall Wilhelm Kietel. This organization was closer in function to the US Joint Chiefs of Staff than to SHAEF, but the OKW's powers were substantially circumscribed by Hitler. In the wake of the July 20, 1944, bomb plot, Hitler lost confidence in the loyalty of the senior Army commanders and took greater and greater operational and tactical control of the war effort.

The closest counterpart to SHAEF was Oberbefehlshaber West, or OB-West (High Command West). However, this was an Army command, not a joint command. OB-West lacked control over Luftwaffe and Kriegsmarine units in the western theater, which had their own separate regional commands. There were several OB-West commanders during the 1944–45 campaign, though undoubtedly the most important was Generalfeldmarshall Gerd von Rundstedt. The architect of the Wehrmacht's stunning defeat of France in 1940, Rundstedt had been brought back to command the Western Front in the summer of 1943 in anticipation of the Allied invasion. Rundstedt was a general of the old school, highly regarded throughout the Wehrmacht for his professionalism and integrity. Although respected by Hitler for his competence, he was outside the Fuhrer's inner circle because of his blunt honesty about Hitler's increasingly delusional military schemes.

Generalfeldmarschall Gerd von Rundstedt commanded OB West for most of 1944–45, though he was relieved twice by Hitler during the campaign. He is seen here in Augsburg in May 1945 after his surrender with his son, Hans-Gerd, behind him. (NARA)

Rundstedt commanded OB-West on D-Day, and through the initial phase of the Normandy campaign until July 2, 1944, when he was relieved by Hitler for proposing to withdraw German forces to more defensible positions in Normandy out of the range of naval gunfire.

It is difficult to judge Rundstedt's performance in Normandy compared to Eisenhower or Montgomery, as he had far less freedom of action than the Allied commanders and his options were circumscribed by Hitler. He was replaced by Günther Hans von Kluge, a favorite of Hitler for his leadership of the 4. Armee during the envelopment of French forces through the Ardennes in 1940. Kluge had a distinguished record on the Eastern Front but was nicknamed "Clever Hans" for his political opportunism and vacillation. He was aware of earlier plots against Hitler, and was privy to the July 20 plot. In the wake of the Falaise Gap disaster, and expecting to be arrested by the Gestapo for his connections to the assassination attempt, Kluge committed suicide on 18 August. He was replaced temporarily by the commander of Heeresgruppe B, Walter Model. Rundstedt returned to the command of the Western Front on September 5, 1944, and continued to lead it until March 1945, when he was relieved by Hitler again after the capture of the Remagen Bridge. Command of OB-West for the remainder of the war was taken over by Kesselring.

Aside from the organizational differences between SHAEF and the OB-West command, Eisenhower had greater operational flexibility and different constraints. When the OKW plan for the Ardennes offensive was unveiled to Rundstedt, Hitler had annotated it by hand, writing "No Changes." The senior commanders, including Rundstedt and the *Heeregruppen* commanders, had very limited tactical flexibility since permission had to be obtained from Berlin for even the most modest of decisions. Rundstedt did not have the political distractions of conducting a war within an alliance like Kesselring in Tunisia or Eisenhower in the Mediterranean and northwest Europe, but the limitations imposed by Hitler were far more debilitating to the conduct of military operations. All of the major German operations in the west in 1944, including the Mortain offensive in August 1944, the Lorraine offensive in September 1944, and the Ardennes offensive in December 1944, were imposed on OB-West by Hitler, with little opportunity for discourse.

INSIDE THE MIND

Dwight Eisenhower was shaped by the culture of his youth, and molded and reshaped by his early Army experiences. Eisenhower was less flamboyant than his contemporaries like MacArthur, Patton, and Clark, but this was because of an enforced austerity and not a lack of personality. Eisenhower grew up as a middle son in a large family and was not as egocentric as many of his contemporaries. The Mennonite culture of Eisenhower's youth saw austerity in dress and humility in behavior as cardinal virtues. While Eisenhower was no longer a practicing member of the sect, its cultural values were evident decades later. His one contribution to military fashion was the "Ike jacket," a simple adaptation of the common British infantryman's battledress. On the other hand, the religious roots of Eisenhower's personality do not fully explain his remarkable career. His father had strayed from the sect and Ike's parents had instilled an untypical streak of ambition in all their sons. Eisenhower's personality was dominated by a zealous self-discipline. His lack of pretense and his inclination to hide his ambitions behind a smiling facade led many to underestimate his intelligence and drive.

Eisenhower in a portrait taken on April 20, 1943, while Commanding General, North African Theater of Operations, US Army (NATOUSA). (NARA)

Eisenhower's Midwestern upbringing lacked the strong streak of anti-British sentiment that was widespread in America's Eastern establishment well into the 20th century. Several of the senior American commanders, most notably Adm. King and Gen. Clark, had a particularly strong anti-British streak. Eisenhower was largely oblivious to these old antagonisms, which was a positive asset for the role he would play.

West Point sought young men with leadership potential, and fostered it beyond mere academic study. Eisenhower was an avid and competitive football player at West Point, and after his injuries he became a skilled and enthusiastic coach. He was not the first or last American to see football as a metaphor for leadership in warfare, and he wrote that "football perhaps more than any other sport, tends to instill in men the feeling that victory comes through hard – almost slavish – work, team play, self-confidence, and an enthusiasm that amounts to dedication."

Eisenhower was intellectually curious and his early knowledge of warfare and command was shaped by his own self-education in the classics rather than by the lackluster military-history courses offered by West Point at the time. There was a revival of interest in the Roman and Greek classics in late 19th-century America, and

Eisenhower parent's, though not wealthy, were exceptionally well educated for their day and had an ample library at home. In spite of his fascination with military history, the essential pacifism at the heart of Mennonism led him away from the military romanticism of his contemporaries like Patton, MacArthur, or Clark. To Eisenhower military service was an honorable duty, not a glorious adventure. Under his own direction, he might have gone in a more technocratic direction in his military career. He was fascinated by aircraft and eventually received flying lessons, over the objections of his wife. His early experiences with tanks led to insightful essays on the future of land warfare, a futuristic viewpoint that was shared with Patton. His farmer's reverence for hard work and his ability to work well as part of a team pushed him in the direction of staff positions over field commands.

Eisenhower as commanding general of SHAEF, in February 1944. (NARA)

As described earlier, Ike's most essential education in the nature of command was his tutelage under Fox Conner during their stint in the Panama Canal Zone. Conner's lessons left Eisenhower with a pessimistic view of Europe's future, and a conviction that a future European war was likely. While Conner's education provided Eisenhower with more intellectual depth, his study at the Command and General Staff School inculcated him with the contemporary American approach to command and staff issues. One of the commandant's key lectures was a prophetic description of the challenges Eisenhower would face two decades later in trying to create an effective joint command: "A football team composed of individuals of medium ability, indoctrinated in team work and led by a real leader will beat a team of hastily assembled stars, all wanting to carry the ball individually and in eleven different directions."

Eisenhower's introduction into the realm of high politics was his assignment under Douglas MacArthur in the Philippines in the late 1930s. Such a posting was unique in the US Army at the time and provided lessons in dealing with a charismatic and difficult senior commander, as well as the challenges of interfacing with foreign governments. The US Army provided Eisenhower with a string of exceptional opportunities in the 1920s and 1930s, but it was Eisenhower's ambition, dedication, and hard work that converted these opportunities into stepping-stones to senior command.

War in the 20th century was changing enormously in size and depth of operations, which greatly changed the nature of command, particularly at its highest levels. Ulysses Grant in the Civil War typically commanded an army of about 120,000 men. When Eisenhower served as chief of staff for the Third US Army in the Louisiana war games in 1941, it consisted of 240,000 men. In the ETO in 1945 Ike would command five American and three Allied field armies as well as a substantial air and naval component. This was anticipated by more visionary commanders like George Marshall and was one of the reasons that Marshall fostered a strong cadre of young commanders with a strong staff background. Command and control in war was shifting from the traditional romantic style of leadership, where a commander like Napoleon could lead his troops within sight of the battlefield, to a new managerial command style with amplified levels of command remote from the battlefield.

When the AFHQ was created in the Mediterranean in late 1942 under Eisenhower's command, there were few precedents. Eisenhower amusingly described his role to a friend as "a one-time soldier, a pseudo-statesman, a jack-legged politician and a crooked diplomat." Eisenhower had to create a combined headquarters largely from scratch, attempting to meld the divergent staff practices of Britain and the United States in a harmonious whole. American and British staffs were not familiar with each other's practices; American experience with European command practices tended to be French-oriented because of the experience of the AEF in World War I, and the subsequent dispatch of US officers to French war colleges in the inter-war years. Eisenhower fully realized that American and British policies would often be antagonistic, since both sides had fundamental disagreements over grand strategy. He attempted to leave these issues to the levels of command above him, namely the CCS, and above them Roosevelt and Churchill. His focus was on reducing the inevitable friction that would occur when attempting to meld the divergent British and American staff practices, seasoned by divergent tactical approaches and divergent strategic goals. His administrative approach was purely pragmatic and attempted to overcome national differences by enforced mingling of staffs.

Aside from the organizational friction that had to be overcome, Eisenhower also faced the inevitable personal discord that naturally occurred when forcing talented and ambitious men from several nations to work together under the stress of war. His personal approach to leadership was to build consensus. Churchill later recalled that "he supervised everything with a vigilant eye, and no one knew better than he how to stand close to a tremendous event without impairing the authority he had delegated to others." Eisenhower also tried to convey some of his own gregarious and jovial persona to his headquarters, insisting on an atmosphere of cheerful confidence. This was not a Pollyannaish over-optimism, but an appreciation that the tasks facing AFHQ and later SHAEF were so daunting that excessive expressions of doubt would only add one more source of friction.

Eisenhower's cardinal rule for American officers was that there was to be no disparagement of the British. There was an apocryphal tale often repeated during the war that Eisenhower sent an American officer back to the States, not because he had called a British colleague a "son-of-a-bitch" but because he had called him a "British son-of-a-bitch."

Eisenhower seen shortly after receiving his fifth star on February 1, 1945, wearing the insignia of the SHAEF command. (NARA)

The frequent criticism that Eisenhower lacked battlefield experience revealed a lack of understanding about his role. The conductor is not necessarily the best musician in an orchestra, and the essential skills for theater command are not the same as for a tactical commander. Eisenhower's preferred metaphor for his role was that of a chairman of the board, an apt comparison in an age that saw the culmination of the industrialization of warfare. Eisenhower's leadership style a decade later during the presidency was later dubbed "the hidden hand." Eisenhower attempted to remain an unobtrusive and conciliatory leader, leaving it up to his key staff to enforce his policies. Eisenhower's personality traits often deceived those who did not know him well. His gregariousness and broad grin disguised a far more veiled and complicated man who operated with such subtlety that his actions were not often appreciated by the casual observer.

WHEN WAR IS DONE

Eisenhower's post-war military career spanned more than a decade, first as the senior American commander and later as president in 1953–1960. This period was marked by a revolution in warfare, with the advent of nuclear weapons and the dawn of the Cold War following the collapse of the wartime alliance in 1945–47. Because of the obvious space limitations in this book, this portion of his career can be only briefly sketched.

Following the German surrender on May 8, 1945, Eisenhower became military governor of the American Zone of Occupation. This post was very short-lived, as in November 1945 he was appointed as Army chief of staff, replacing the retiring George C. Marshall. Marshall later went on to become a distinguished Secretary of State in the Truman administration and was responsible for the famous Marshall Plan, which helped in the reconstruction of war-ravaged Western Europe. During his tenure as Army chief of staff, Eisenhower focused on issues related to Army demobilization, service unification, and the desegregation of the armed forces. The AAF was pushing for autonomy from the Army, which Eisenhower supported, while at the same time he was part of the effort to reorganize the War Department as a unified and modernized Department of Defense. Army desegregation had been foreshadowed by Eisenhower's own actions in 1945, when he had accepted African-Americans into previously segregated infantry divisions.

With his retirement approaching, Eisenhower received the entreaties of both political parties to join their ranks as a gubernatorial or senatorial candidate.

The toll of time. A portrait of Ike at the beginning of American involvement in the war in December 1941, and shortly after the war in 1946. (NARA)

Eisenhower had remained deliberately apolitical when in uniform, and showed no immediate enthusiasm for a political career. During a meeting with his old boss Douglas MacArthur in 1946, Eisenhower asked whether he planned to run for president in 1948. MacArthur replied that one or the other of them would become president, but that he was too old. When Ike retorted that he had no such ambitions, MacArthur replied: "That's right, Ike. You go on like that and you'll get it for sure!"

When offered the presidency of Columbia University in 1947, he indicated that he would accept once he was officially released from his duties as Army chief of staff; when he left the position on February 6, 1948, Bradley took his place. Eisenhower was ill suited to this figurehead and fund-raising position, and was gradually dragged back into national affairs because of the turmoil over the unification of the armed services. Secretary of Defense James Forrestal was floundering in the new position and requested that Eisenhower return to Washington in January 1949 to become a consultant on defense affairs. In February 1949 President Harry Truman asked him to become chairman of the Joint Chiefs of Staff in order to provide a respected authority to lead the troubled unification efforts, as well as to chart a strategic course as relations with the Soviet Union worsened. The pressure to return to national life increased in 1950 after the outbreak of the Korean War. The acceleration of the Cold War led to the creation of the new North Atlantic Treaty Organization (NATO) in April 1949, but it was bedeviled by the substantial demilitarization after the war as well as difficult strategic decisions such as the issue of German remilitarization. In December 1950 Eisenhower returned to uniform and was appointed as Supreme Allied Commander Europe (SACEUR).

Eisenhower faced the challenge of creating a viable defense plan for Western Europe in the face of very restricted resources. Although the European economies had begun to recover, there was widespread reluctance to mobilize significant national resources so soon after the last war. The stalemate in the Korean War by 1951 and growing American casualties there had undermined political support for the Truman administration. With national elections approaching in 1952, Eisenhower was increasingly badgered to abandon his apolitical stance and throw in his hat with the Republican Party. He was deeply disturbed that the Republican nomination would likely go to Robert A. Taft, who favored an isolationist American foreign policy. At this critical time, Eisenhower felt that isolationism was a dangerous course, and that Truman was so unpopular that Taft was likely to be elected president. In the event, Truman decided against running again, and the Democrats nominated Adlai Stevenson. Eisenhower threw his hat in the ring, won the Republican nomination, and then the

The difficulties in the early formative years of NATO encouraged Truman to ask for Eisenhower's help. Here he is seen with some familiar faces but in new roles with the Standing Group of NATO on January 31, 1951. Bradley to the left was US representative at the time while Lord Tedder was UK representative. Behind them from left to right are Vice Admiral Jerauld Wright (deputy US representative), Général Paul Ely (French representative), and Lieutenant-General Alfred Gruenther (chief of staff, Supreme HQ Allied Powers Europe). (NARA)

presidency in November 1952. Eisenhower's politics were moderate, favoring an internationalist foreign policy, prudent federal spending, and moderately liberal social policies including efforts to end segregation. In 1952, he remarked that "every gun that is made, every warship launched, every rocket fired signifies in the final sense, a theft from those who hunger and are not fed, those who are cold and are not yet clothed... Under the cloud of threatening war, it is humanity hanging from an iron cross." These were hardly the words of a conventional militarist.

Eisenhower was relieved by the death of Josef Stalin and a three-year period of turmoil in the Soviet leadership, which muted Cold War tensions. The Korean War ended in stalemate in 1953. Eisenhower's foreign policy tried to convince the American public of the necessity of the United States taking a global leadership role. Eisenhower did not favor careless entanglements in regional conflicts, staying aloof from the French trouble in Indochina, but his administration did take action when deemed necessary, whether discouraging Anglo-French involvement in the Suez crisis in 1956 or intervening in the crises over Taiwan and Lebanon. In the military sphere, Eisenhower wanted to provide greater funding for the Department of Defense than it had under the Truman administration, but at the same time he did not view this as a blank check to the military. The "New Look" policy adopted by the military placed greater reliance on tactical nuclear weapons, but the policy was a subtle way of minimizing the size of the Army's conventional forces rather than trying to match the bloated size of the Soviet ground forces. He regarded the cost of American military power as a cruel necessity and the price that had to be paid for security and prosperity. Eisenhower expanded American intelligence activities as an alternative means of fostering US interests. Eisenhower's calm and prudent tenure was followed by a decade of turmoil under the Kennedy and Johnson administrations, which floundered through the Cuban crises and the morass of the Vietnam War; it is hard to imagine Eisenhower becoming entangled in either.

Eisenhower made a campaign pledge in 1952 to go to Korea to discover how to end the war there. He is seen here alongside Major-General James Fry on December 6, 1952, visiting the troops. Stalin's death in March 1953 cleared the way for the eventual armistice. (NARA)

A LIFE IN WORDS

Eisenhower never wrote a full autobiography, and his most memorable book was his account of the war, *Crusade in Europe*, published in 1948. A fine account of the origins of the memoir by Professor Manfred Jonas of Union College can be found in the 1979 De Capo paperback edition. *Crusade in Europe* proved to be a popular bestseller. Like Eisenhower himself, the book is an unadorned account of the campaign in Europe from his perspective. It is largely lacking in criticism of other senior Allied commanders in spite

Outgoing president Harry Truman meets Eisenhower on the day of his inauguration – January 20, 1953 – in front of the White House. (NARA)

of their wartime differences. Ike had been given the opportunity to review portions of Pershing's memoirs in the 1920s, and he felt it was demeaning for senior commanders to settle old scores in their memoirs. His memoir was also constrained by the year it was written in, 1948, which made it impossible for Eisenhower to discuss many of the intelligence aspects of his key decision-making, most notably Ultra. Besides this memoir, Eisenhower's papers have been published in a multi-volume set, and excerpts from his diaries have also been published. One of the most interesting collections of his writings is *Dear General*, which contains his most important correspondence with Marshall during the war.

The Pogue volume *The Supreme Command* in the US Army Green Book series of official histories is the official account of SHAEF, and this is an organizational portrait rather than a biographical treatment of Eisenhower. Four of Eisenhower's associates wrote wartime accounts. Walter Bedell Smith's *Eisenhower's Six Great Decisions* provides thumbnail sketches of the key command decisions in the ETO and explains their rationales. A far more personal picture of Eisenhower emerges from Harry Butcher's memoir of the war years. This work was extremely controversial at the time, as it was the first to expose Ike's fractious relations with Montgomery and Churchill. Indeed, Eisenhower thought that Butcher had betrayed his trust, and it ended their friendship. His driver, Kay Summersby, followed in 1948 with *Eisenhower Was My Boss*, which provided a fresh but less controversial peek into SHAEF headquarters during the war years. The most detailed personal account of the command decisions within SHAEF in 1944–45 is Arthur Tedder's memoir. As a senior RAF officer, Tedder had extensive access to the senior ranks of the British general staff and was present at most of the key discussions at SHAEF. His recollections lean towards the controversies over the use of air power, which offers a refreshing change from most accounts, which center on the debates over army operations.

Passing on the torch to a new generation. President-elect John Kennedy confers with President Eisenhower in the White House on December 6, 1960, before his inauguration. (NARA)

Considering the importance of Eisenhower's command as well as his post-war career as president, it is not surprising that there are numerous biographies as well as a fine selection of specialized monographs. A number of the biographies, such as those by Ambrose, D'Este, and Perret, are by some of America's finest military historians. The excellent account by Eisenhower's grandson David provides an especially detailed account of the war years. Another essential work is the recent Crosswell biography of "Eisenhower's bulldog," Walter Bedell Smith, which provides considerable insight into the wartime command controversies.

FURTHER READING

Government Studies

Organization of the European Theater of Operations (General Board Study No. 2: 1946)

Evolution of a Theater of Operations Headquarters 1941–1967 (Combat Operations Research Group: 1967)

History of AFHQ (AFHQ: 1945)

Books

Ambrose, Stephen, *Eisenhower and Berlin 1945: The Decision to Halt at the Elbe* (Norton: 1967)

——, *The Supreme Commander: The War Years of General Dwight Eisenhower* (Doubleday: 1970)

Bedell Smith, Walter, *Eisenhower's Six Great Decisions: Europe 1944–45* (Curtis: 1946)

Butcher, Harry, *My Three Years with Eisenhower* (Simon & Schuster: 1946)

Crosswell, D. K. R., *Beetle: The Life of General Walter Bedell Smith* (University Press of Kentucky: 2010)

Eisenhower, David, *Eisenhower at War 1943–45* (Random House: 1986)

Eisenhower, Dwight, *Crusade in Europe* (Doubleday: 1948)

Eisenhower, John S. D., *General Ike: A Personal Reminiscence* (Free Press: 2003)

D'Este, Carlo, *Eisenhower: A Soldier's Life* (Henry Holt: 2002)

Ferrell, Robert (ed.), *The Eisenhower Diaries* (Norton: 1981)

Gelb, Norman, *Ike & Monty: Generals at War* (Morrow: 1994)

Greenfield, Kent (ed.), *Command Decisions* (Harcourt, Brace: 1959)

Hobbs, Joseph, *Dear General: Eisenhower's Wartime Letters to Marshall* (John Hopkins: 1971)

Holland, Matthew, *Eisenhower Between the Wars: The Making of a General and Statesman* (Praeger: 2001)

Jablonsky, David, *War by Land, Sea, and Air: Dwight Eisenhower and the Concept of Unified Command* (Yale: 2010)

Korda, Michael, *Ike: An American Hero* (Harper: 2007)

Larrabee, Eric, *Commander and Chief: Franklin Delano Roosevelt, His Lieutenants, and their War* (Naval Institute: 1987)

Miller, Merle, *Ike the Soldier: As They Knew Him* (Putnam's: 1987)

Perret, Geoffrey, *Eisenhower* (Random House: 1999)

Perry, Mark, *Partners in Command: George Marshall and Dwight Eisenhower in War and Peace* (Penguin: 2007)

Pogue, Forrest, *The Supreme Command* (Center for Military History: 1954)

Tedder, Arthur, *With Prejudice* (Little, Brown: 1966)

Terzian, Philip, *Architects of Power: Roosevelt, Eisenhower and the American Century* (Encounter: 2010)

INDEX